Read what these famous writers are saying about the most controversial issues of our time!

". . . if Luther and Calvin considered (not without
cause, as the Roman Catholic Counter-Reformation showed)
the Christianity of the medieval church deformed,
it is questionable whether they would consider the religion
of their 'Protestant' successors in the mid twentieth
century Christianity at all."

Harold O. J. Brown, Part II

"The Catholic Church is, by common understanding, the
bastion of resistance, because of its widely recognized stand
against 'birth control.' In fact the Catholic Church is
busily re-examining the premises of existing
regulations on the subject."

Wm. F. Buckley Jr., Part IV

"It has been argued that only well-educated Catholics
appreciate the Mass in Latin. This I know to be untrue but even
if it were true the Universal Church in her charity
should find a modest niche even for all the well-educated."

Sir Arnold Lunn, Part VI

Other famous authors you will
read in this book . . .

Evelyn Waugh   *Will Herberg*   *Jeffrey Hart*

Russell Kirk   *L. Brent Bozell*   *Garry Wills*

Alice-Leone Moats   *Thomas Molnar*   *Marvin R. O'Connell*

Frederick D. Wilhelmsen   *Erik von Kuehnelt-Leddihn*

DEDICATION

O Lord, who appears to us as the origin and reward of truth, grant Your protection to all here this evening who have pursued the truth. We thank you for the accomplishments of this last decade and we ask without pretension for high graces in the next decade. Give us perception and judgment, strengthen our integrity, and grant us the subtle grace of balance to be able to pursue truth and political advantage without loss to either, to strike hard where we should without anger, even to shatter calumny without passion, and to lead a popular following responsibly. And in all to serve Your people of every temperament and station, looking not to their gratitude but to Your approval only. Lord bless particularly the directors and writers of NR, plus its readers, and bless, in the tradition You have taught us, its critics and worst enemies Amen.

(Invocation given by the Rev. Eugene V. Clark at the 10th Anniversary Dinner of **National Review**, *November 11, 1965*

THE
REBIRTH OF
CHRIST

*and other essays
on religion from*
NATIONAL REVIEW

Edited and Introduced by J. P. McFadden

National Review Inc.
New York City • 1966

a National Review

CURRENT EVENTS book

CONTENTS

Introduction

"Perhaps," said my friend, "people want to find out whether Heaven will be better than the Great Society."

He was joking about something both of us found difficult to explain: the new—and amazing—revival of interest in religion among Americans of *all* faiths. It is this new and vital interest that provides the reason for this book.

Not many years ago, the average American considered religion (if indeed, he considered it at all) a private matter. Today television, newspapers and magazines devote enormous amounts of space to religious debates and discussions.

Why? The reasons are many, and no doubt have much to do with the realization that political, economic or scientific solutions cannot solve all the problems that trouble our world. If a single *individual* is responsible, it is Pope John: who said that the idea for the Ecumenical Council came to him as a "sudden inspiration." Something like that seems to have inspired religious leaders everywhere to re-examine basic beliefs. To say that this has produced startling results would be gross understate-

ment: the "new look" includes everything from a notice-
able alteration in Rome's approach to Communism, to
Protestantism's growing *rapprochment* with Catholicism
(and *vice versa*), and on to an English Bishop's declaration that "God is dead," and an American's doubting the
divinity of Christ (see Part V).

Meanwhile, whereas Catholics and Protestants and
Jews nowadays seem to get along much better with each
other, they seem to get along less well among *themselves*.
Much of the controversy in this book is *intra*, not *inter*-
denominational.

The chapters that make up this book were first published in the pages of *National Review*, most of them
during the past year. At first, the editors were hesitant
to publish many articles about religion: secular magazines
usually leave the subject to the religious journals. When,
in December 1962, NR published "The Same Again,
Please," the late Evelyn Waugh's study of the prospects
for the just-beginning Ecumenical Council, we were un-
prepared for the reaction.

Thousands of readers—not just bishops, priests and
ministers, but mainly laymen—wrote to request additional
copies. An archbishop mailed it to every Catholic bishop
in America. A woman in St. Louis asked "How much
would it cost to mail Mr. Waugh's fine article to the en-
closed list of ministers?", naming over a thousand. Along
with the praise came strong criticism: Catholics charged
us with "vicious" and "reactionary" attacks on Pope
John and the Council; Protestants accused us of being
"too Catholic," even "Popish."

We discovered something else that was strange. Most
of the strictly political controversies in *National Review*
have short, vigorous lives, and then subside, to be re-
placed by new ones. Not so here. With each succeeding
article, interest increased. Nor was it unusual for someone to write, a year later, to ask for "a copy of the
thing you published about the gnostics on the train."
Reprinting followed reprinting, and while the demand
didn't seem great at any one time, always the copies were
spoken for, and back to press we would go for another
lot.

Thereupon *National Review* published a special issue,
with a number of articles grouped under the title "What,

In the Name of God, Is Going On In the Catholic Church?", followed by another article called "The Protestant Deformation."

Both issues produced a flood of mail, and—significantly—were near sell-outs on newsstands. And now readers wanted copies not just of one or the other, but of both together.

The most explosive of all was the Birth Control issue. Here, of course, religious convictions get mixed with political ones, and the debate grew hot. Garry Wills' article seemed reasonable and measured to us, but for some weeks thereafter our mailbag had a distinctive red glow. (This time, not so many people wanted copies— just the opportunity to have a good fight through the mails.)

Finally came one of the most impressive articles *National Review* has ever published: Jeffrey Hart's brilliant "The Rebirth of Christ." Mr. Hart is well-known to NR readers for his new book, "The American Dissent," which traces the history of modern American conservatism. What you will read here is the initial study for yet another book (on C. S. Lewis) which Professor Hart is now writing.

It is safe to predict that any Christian—indeed, anyone interested in religion at all—will enjoy this one. It was the enthusiastic reception of "The Rebirth of Christ" that produced the idea (as well as the title) for this book. One morning I saw a letter that concluded: "Of *all* the articles you have published about religion, *this* one is the *best*!"

All the articles! Why not?

Thus the book you have in your hand: the best articles from *National Review* on the current controversy involving religion—written by Protestant, Catholic and Jewish contributors—here together in one ecumenical offering.

You will find a wide variety of ideas and viewpoints. Happily they lend themselves to congenial grouping. First, Mr. Hart makes the most important point of all: religion is being rapidly established as a force among *intellectuals*—those whose opinions determine what the *future* will believe. So while it may be true that today's "Common Man" has lost the "feel" of religion, his children (and yours!) are likely to re-discover it.

Then we have a look at Christianity today, first by Professor Harold O. J. Brown, himself an ordained minister, who brilliantly analyzes the decline of traditional Protestantism; followed by Professor Garry Wills, who looks with considerable awe at the enormous changes taking place in Roman Catholicism (and concludes that ours is, at the very least, an *exciting* age for Catholics).

The section entitled *The Christian in the Modern World* is introduced by the renowned sociologist Will Herberg, who begins with an eloquent statement of the place of religion in public life, and the urgent *need* for it. Mr. Russell Kirk (teacher, newspaper columnist, novelist, and author of several famous volumes on political philosophy) contributes a scorching denunciation of those who would eliminate all religion from our public schools. The scholar-journalist, Erik von Kuehnelt-Leddihn, provides a fascinating look at the Christian as social sentimentalist, followed by Mr. Herberg again, who asks pertinent questions about whether civil rights advocates have any religiously derived "right" to violate the law. Finally, Frederick D. Wilhelmsen tears into a new book by young Catholics who find much to sneer at in their own Church (". . . Ottaviani, relics . . . McCarthy, rosary, Spellman . . . The Knights of Columbus . . .") but have lost sight of the menace organized atheism (e.g., world Communism) is to any religion, however modernized.

Part IV deals with one of the most controversial issues of our time: birth control. First Wm. F. Buckley Jr. sets before us the measure and seriousness of the problem. Then Mr. Wills takes the hot coal in his hands. His article was originally published as part of "The Population Explosion," a *National Review* supplement dealing with the general subject in depth. But it was the religious aspect that provoked the sharpest rebuttal. L. Brent Bozell's reply to Wills is not only representative of the other side in this still-continuing debate, but also comes from an accomplished writer and polemicist who is considered a leading spokesman for the Catholic Right. Wills (who writes a column which is syndicated nationally in the Catholic press) has the last word here, but you will no doubt be hearing further from Bozell.

No theological controversy in years has provoked such widespread international interest as the one centered on

English Bishop John Robinson's *Honest to God,* which proclaims the death of the traditional God of Christianity. Harold O. J. Brown reviews that book, and makes some penetrating insights into what it all means, and not just from the Protestant point of view ("Lest other Christians, notably Roman Catholics, too glibly rejoice [that Robinson's thesis is a strictly Protestant problem], let it be pointed out that the [book's] theology . . . is now turning up in the oddest places . . . even at the Vatican Council"). Next Sir Arnold Lunn, the Catholic layman, author and sportsman (he "invented" skiing's slalom) gives the inside story of the *New Morality* Bishop Robinson and his friends are promoting. Sir Arnold speaks from personal knowledge both of the controversy and many of the principle figures involved. (In fact, he has, in collaboration with an Anglican, Garth Lean, written two books on the subject.)

Part VI is devoted to *The Council,* Pope John's "sudden inspiration" that changed the religious climate of our world. Evelyn Waugh leads off. With vivid and dramatic insight, Waugh puts Vatican II in historical perspective. Although written before the Council's first session, it is as informative and readable today as when first published.

The four articles that follow deal with various aspects of the controversies stirred up by the deliberations of the Council Fathers. We hear again from Dr. Herberg and Mr. Bozell. Catholic readers will no doubt find Professor Thomas Molnar's contribution disturbing, his thesis being that the "Aggiornamento" we are experiencing is not quite what Pope John had in mind. Alice-Leone Moats, who spends much of her time in Italy, reports on some of the reasons why Pope Paul found John a difficult man to follow. Finally, Sir Arnold Lunn, who was in Rome at the closing, sums up the Council: what it did, and what it left undone.

So read on. You will find good writing, copious information, and new ideas. I suspect that some of you will find yourselves in disagreement, more or less violent, with much in it. It has been a revelation for me to witness the extraordinary interest in the ideas—so sincerely and passionately put down—of these writings on subjects considered, not long ago, as fit mainly for the classroom or

the seminary. Clearly religious discussion is back in style.
Perhaps we are indeed entering, where religion is concerned, the "post-modern" world.

It should be a *better* world. To celebrate it, I have
taken the liberty of tucking into the back of this book
two little pieces that should amuse you. "Gnostics on a
Train" is by a Catholic priest (using a pen name here,
naturally!), and is just plain funny. "Notes toward a
Grammar" is "Fritz" Wilhelmsen at his Bellocian best:
a bare-knuckled, raucous lampoon of that great modern
vogue, The Dialogue. God knows it is true that today we
think too little of the *hereafter*; perhaps because there is
so little to laugh at in the here-and-now. Hopefully, this
little book will contribute something of value in both
directions.

J. P. McFADDEN

The Rebirth
of Christ

I

THINKERS LOOK UP

The Rebirth of Christ

JEFFREY HART

As a scholar, C. S. Lewis simply knew too much to remain a prisoner of the Spirit of the Age, to succumb to the appeal of the merely fashionable.[1] He was completely liberated from chronological snobbery. He did not suppose a statement true because it had been made recently, or because people around him seemed to accept it. "I take a very low view of 'climates of opinion,'" he wrote. "In his own subject every man knows that all discoveries are made and all errors corrected by those who ignore the 'climate of opinion.'" And beyond this, Lewis learned, by studying earlier periods and examining their assumptions, to become aware of what Whitehead calls the "of courses" of culture—the things everyone assumes to have been proved, or to be self-evidently true, and therefore leaves unexamined. Lewis condemned "the uncritical acceptance of the intellectual climate common to our

---

[1] To most university students and their professors, C. S. Lewis is well known as a scholar and literary critic. His two books on medieval literature, his books on Milton and on sixteenth-century literature, and his widely ranging essays, have firmly established his authority in the Academy. Such scholarly and critical work has its independent importance, of course, quite apart from his other writing; and, indeed, those students and professors who admire him in this aspect are very likely to be only marginally aware of him as he appears to the broad reading public: a *phenomenally* popular writer on religious subjects.

3

own age and the assumption that whatever has gone out of date is on that account discredited. You must find why it went out of date. Was it ever refuted (and if so by whom, where, and how conclusively) or did it merely die away as fashions do? If the latter, this tells us nothing about its truth or falsehood. From seeing this, one passes to the realization that our own age is also a 'period,' and certainly has, like all periods, its own characteristic illusions. They are likely to lurk in those widespread assumptions that are so ingrained in the age that no one dares to attack or feels it necessary to defend them."

Surely such liberation from present-mindedness is one of the main reasons—it may even, finally, be *the* main reason—for studying history or literature.[2] In Lewis' last book, *The Discarded Image*, the way in which historical study has a liberating effect appears with particular clarity. This book, published posthumously, consists of a series of lectures he delivered several times in his course at Cambridge, and it deals with the medieval conception, or "image" as the title has it, of the universe. Lewis explains that the Middle Ages were neither "primitive" nor "scientific" but "bookish." They were quite unlike the primitive society, in which culture is absorbed, often unconsciously, through participation in age-old habits of behavior. Nor were they scientific in the modern sense. Rather, they built up their image of the universe out of the works of older authors, usually classical, but also Judaic, Patristic, Stoic and Neo-Platonic, brought together over a long period of time to form "a single, complex, harmonious mental model of the universe" which was able to accommodate their science, history, and theology. This model is fairly familiar in its outlines. At the center is the earth—spherical, of course; the idea that the Middle Ages thought the earth was flat is entirely false—and the earth is surrounded by a series of transparent globes, one above the other. Fixed in each of

[2] We become aware that we have assumptions, and that they *are* assumptions; and we develop a similar awareness about our behavior. In the past men have been, variously, more sensuous, more brutal, more ceremonius, more pious, more ascetic, than they seem to be at present. They may well be so again. The past is thus both liberating intellectually and a reservoir of moral possibility. And this is the unanswerable argument for establishing literacy and historical study as the foundation for education. By their very nature, and useful as they are, mathematics and science do not produce the same effect.

those spheres is a luminous body, a planet. Further out comes the *stellatum*, the sphere of the stars, and finallly the *Primum Mobile*, or First Mover, itself invisible, but, moved by its love of God, imparting movement to all the inner spheres. Beyond the *Primum Mobile* we move outside space and time altogether, into a realm of pure intellectual light—Heaven.

This model has been described in a great many books on medieval thought and literature, but when Lewis deals with it some very special things occur. First, he can so involve himself with the model that he can communicate a sense of how it felt to live in it. He knows the philosophers, historians, and poets so well that he can, so to speak, see with their eyes. Without such involvement, indeed—of this kind, if not to this degree— literary and historical study cannot have the liberating effect of which I spoke: the thing must really be known, and not merely guessed at. Speaking of the medieval universe, Lewis tells us that the "human imagination has seldom had before it an object so sublimely ordered," and that medieval space, unlike ours, was neither dark nor silent. "The sun illuminates the whole universe; night is merely the conical shadow cast by the earth, and it turns through the brilliantly lighted universe like the hand of a clock." Beyond that, the spheres as they turn produce harmonious music. How did it feel to inhabit such a universe? To "look out on the night sky with modern eyes is like looking out over a sea that fades away in the mist. . . . To look up at the towering medieval universe is more like looking up at a great building." Our "universe is romantic and theirs was classical." Or again: in "modern, that is, in evolutionary thought Man stands at the top of a stair whose foot is lost in obscurity; in this, he stands at the bottom of a stair whose top is invisible with light." But though Lewis knows that this model gave, and can still give, aesthetic pleasure—the same sort of pleasure one gets from Dante or the *Summa* or Chartres: the experience of diversity harmoniously contained—he is so intensely involved with it that he can feel its limitations as well. It was sublimely ordered, but "if it has an aesthetic fault, it is perhaps, for us who have known romanticism, a shade too ordered. For all its vast spaces it might in the end afflict us with a kind of claustrophobia. Is there nowhere any vagueness? No undiscovered by-ways? No twilight? Can we never get really out of doors?"

But if Lewis knows and can communicate what it felt like to live inside the model, he knows other things as well. He knows that in many respects medieval thought was highly sophisticated. No more than a modern theologian, for example, did St. Jerome hold every sentence of the Old Testament to be scientific or historical truth. He said that Moses described Creation "after the manner of a popular poet," or, as we would say, "mythically." Lewis knows that symbolism, and a subtle sense of the relations between symbols and facts, are not something we have discovered recently. The Middle Ages, for example, believed in the existence of three hierarchies of angels, each hierarchy consisting of three different kinds.[3] The scheme derived from a writer known as the pseudo-Dionysius. A modern writer, with a good deal of bad nineteenth-century art in mind, would consider the entire system clear proof of medieval fatuity. But Lewis points out that these angels of course were *celestial* beings, and that "educated people in the Middle Ages never believed the winged men who represent angels in painting and sculpture to be more than symbols." Even the vast intricate model of the universe itself, he points out, had a symbolic quality. "The great masters do not take any model quite so seriously as the rest of us. They know that it is, after all, only a model, possibly replaceable."

In that last sentence, Lewis' phrase "the rest of us" can be only a lecturer's courtesy, for the point he is making is in fact the main one to emerge from *The Discarded Image*. Our mental models of reality are metaphors, and not reality itself; and beyond that, they are cultural productions, as much the constructions of imagination as a poem or a sonata. Models of the universe change be-

---

[3] For those with a taste for information of this sort, there were the Seraphim, Cherubim and Thrones; the Dominations, Powers and Virtues; and the Princedoms, Archangels and Angels. Lewis is an acute critic of the representation of angels in literature. Dante's angels, he says, have "unrivalled majesty," but Milton, "aiming at that, missed the target. Classicism had come in between. His angels have too much anatomy and too much armour, are too much like the gods of Homer and Virgil, and (for that very reason) far less like the gods of paganism in its highest religious development. After Milton total degredation sets in and we finally reach the purely consolatory, hence waterishly feminine, angels of nineteenth-century art." (*The Discarded Image*, p. 75)

cause "nature gives most of her evidence in response to the questions we ask her." Or, elsewhere: "What we learn from experience depends on the kind of philosophy we bring to experience." As he points out, it is possible to trace historically the human demand for a developing, or "modern," universe back into the eighteenth century. When the demand "is full grown the scientists go to work and discover the evidence on which our belief in that sort of universe would now be held to rest. . . . Nature has all sorts of phenomena in stock and can suit many different tastes." Lewis' contention is not, of course, that the universe does not develop. It does. But that our stress on the fact is cultural. A hierarchical arrangement of the evidence is perfectly conceivable. Even the old cosmology accommodated the facts and might actually still do so: the "old astronomy was not in any exact sense 'refuted' by the telescope. The scarred surface of the Moon and the satellites of Jupiter can, if one wants, be fitted into a geocentric scheme. Even the enormous, and enormously different distances of the stars can be accommodated if you are prepared to make their sphere, the *stellatum*, of a vast thickness."

As we come to the end of these lectures, we realize that we have witnessed a breathtaking piece of intellectual virtuosity. Lewis' point of course, is not that we should attempt to will the medieval cosmology back into being. For some reason any writer who deals with the Middle Ages runs the risk of being charged with a desire to "turn the clock back," and, indeed, Miss Kathleen Nott, an English critic of Leftist and anti-Christian bent has wooden-headedly accused Lewis of such an intention. But Lewis' imaginative sympathy is not to be construed in any such fashion. Did not Tawney observe that sympathy is a catalyst of knowledge? Still less does Lewis mean to argue that Christianity is bound up with the old model. He even points out ways in which the model and the spirit of Christianity are in tension, if not outright conflict. He means, rather, to demonstrate—by describing the model and then stepping outside it—how rooted in assumption *any* model is, and, finally, how rooted in assumption are many attitudes that pass as established truth. This is a theme that recurs again and again in his books. "The moment rational thought ceases," he writes in *Miracles*, "imagination, mental habit, and the 'spirit of the age' take charge of you again. New thoughts, until they have themselves become habitual, will affect your consciousness as a whole only while you are actually thinking them. Reason has but to nod at his post, and instantly Nature's patrols are infiltrating. Therefore . . . the mere gravitation of the mind back to its habitual outlook must be discounted" when we are considering whether a statement is true or false. By inhabiting the medieval consciousness, and then stepping outside it, we practice, so to speak, for performing the same operation with regard to the presuppositions of our own period. Far from being anti-modern, as Miss Nott would have him, Lewis, in his rationalism, in his distrust of habit and established attitude, is (compare him with Burke) almost frighteningly modern. And paradoxically it is this radical skepticism about assumptions, this distrust of received opinion, that gives to his religious writing its special kind of power.

For the point is that as far as religion is concerned the climate of opinion is hostile. As Lewis says in *Miracles*, "we all have Naturalism in our bones. . . . Naturalistic assumptions, beggings of the questions . . . will meet you on every side—even from the pens of clergymen. You must develop a nose like a bloodhound for those steps in the argument which depend not on historical or linguistic knowledge" but on concealed assumptions, and "this means that you must really re-educate yourself: must work hard and consistently to eradicate from your mind the whole type of thought in which we have been brought up." Certainly a large undertaking; but the intention to re-educate, to combat rooted assumption, is central to Lewis' work.

Mr. Edmund Wilson blandly informs us that religious belief is an impossibility for any intelligent modern person, and further, that no intelligent person can now suppose Jesus to have been divine. Wilson himself is intelligent and well-read; his ratiocinative powers are far from contemptible; he would have known at once that both of his statements are completely untrue—if he had paused to examine them. Whether or not religious propositions are true or not, it is simply a matter of fact that men who are both intelligent and modern affirm that they are true; Eliot, Lewis, Maritain, Tate, Auden, Gilson, Waugh, Claudel—all believe precisely those propositions which, Wilson asserts, no intelligent modern person can believe. They are intelligent. They are modern. And Wilson himself knows no pertinent fact they are unaware of. When he made those statements Wilson was acting as a spokesman for the Spirit of Age. He supposed that the assault upon Christianity has been intellectually conclusive merely because it has been, in many places, historically successful. Most intellectual solecisms have moral roots; Wilson's proceeded from a form of success worship. At one time, as the elderly devil Screwtape writes to his nephew Wormwood in *The Screwtape Letters*, men "knew pretty well when a thing was proved and when it was not; and if it was proved they really believed it." But "with the weekly press and other such weapons we have largely altered that." They now do not "think of doctrines as primarily 'true' or 'false,' but as 'academic' or 'practical,' 'outworn' or 'contemporary,' 'conventional' or 'ruthless.' " If the average intellectual during the Middle Ages did not really entertain the idea that Christianity might be false, the average intellectual today does not really entertain the idea that it might be true. He does not ask those essential questions, so insisted upon by Lewis: "Was it ever refuted (and if so by whom, where, and how conclusively) or did it merely die away as fashions do? If the latter, this tells us nothing about its truth or falsehood." But of course it takes a remarkable man, and a remarkably free one, to insist upon those questions.

The explanation of how a climate of opinion hostile or indifferent to Christianity came to be established cannot be attempted here. And it is no doubt symptomatic that we lack a genuine history (and I do not mean a self-congratulatory account of the advance of the Light) of the emergence of naturalism—a history that would investigate it in its significant sociological, psychological, political, and economic aspects. In a recent book, John Courtney Murray has distinguished between "the aristocratic atheism of the seventeenth and eighteenth centuries" and "the bourgeois atheism of the nineteenth century." The first was an attempt to understand the world, the second to make money in it. And both were deeply

involved with politics. "The aristocratic atheism of the
French Enlightenment . . . embodied a political will. The
attack on religion—more exactly on the Catholic faith
and on the status of the Church in public life—had as one
of its important purposes to undermine the status of the
king, to clear the way for a direct attack upon the absolute monarchy, which was supported by the power of the
Church. Similarly, a political will lay behind the bourgeois atheism of the nineteenth century. Across its hostility to religion ran the intention of eradicating the
remnants of feudalism—the power of the Restoration
monarchies, the privileges of the nobility, the wealth of
the great landowners—which, again, stood in close relationship to the ecclesiastical order. In the seventeenth
and eighteenth and even in the nineteenth centuries, you
could not touch religion without touching politics—and
vice versa." Thus the emergence of anti-religious thought
was in resonance with powerful political and economic
tendencies, was in harmony with the spirit of the age.
And when an argument is thus in resonance with powerful
historical tendencies it receives a great deal of unearned
power.[4]

When we examine as closely as we can the process by
which the "climate of opinion" actually became established, some remarkable things emerge. The closeness of
the examination is important, because it is *specialized*
knowledge that seems to be the most effective weapon
against assumption and erroneous if widespread opinion.
In the study of history, for example, intensive research
on limited areas has exploded most of the assumptions
reflected in nineteenth-century history books or in such
broad popular surveys as H. G. Wells' *Outline of History*.
But though such specialized knowledge does, I suppose,
diffuse itself in society, the process is at best a slow one.

---

[4] Hume's *Essay on Miracles*, for example, was celebrated and influential,
despite the fact that its utter circularity appears at once to the disin-
terested glance. Hume begins by arguing that nature is uniform to a
very high degree of probability, and concludes that miracles (interrup-
tions of nature) are highly improbable—that is, he concludes that nature
is very uniform to a very high degree of probability. This is not to
mention the appropriateness of the probability criterion here: no one
has ever claimed that miracles are probable, and indeed the very idea
of a probable miracle is itself contradictory. Furthermore, a unique
event can scarcely be either probable or improbable. It either occurred
or it did not. As Lewis himself remarks, the existence of the universe
is a unique event: does that mean it is improbable?

How many of us actually know, with any degree of certainty, the state of knowledge on matters outside our immediate field—even on matters of great importance? How many people actually know very much about the state of knowledge on the question of the historical reliability of the synoptic Gospels? Are they, in the view of sober scholars today, mostly myth? Works of fiction? Is Christ a corn-god?

Now everyone knows that during the nineteenth century, particularly in Germany, the text of the Bible was subjected to sustained and vigorous analysis. Such men as Paulus, Reinhard, Hase, Strauss, Renan, and the two Bauers devoted their lives to the study. But beyond the feeling that this analysis somehow damaged the credibility of the Gospels, how many people now know what these critics actually said, or how many of their points still stand? We recall that Arnold spoke of "all the science of Tubingen," meaning the most important and influential school of German Biblical criticism, and that he considered it a model of scientific method. Through the writings of such literary figures as Arnold and George Eliot, the view gained currency that the Tubingen school was a formidable authority. But what, in fact, has been the fate of its scholarship? The best modern scholarship now asserts that vital parts of the German criticism rested "on no evidence whatsoever, and belong purely to the realm of fancy." Ironically enough, in view of Arnold's opinion, it was English scholarship, carried forward by Lightfoot, Westcott, Hort and others which was decisive in destroying the position of Tubingen. It is now clear that Ferdinand Bauer, the greatest of the Tubingen scholars, as well as his followers, was fatally in error about the dating of the New Testament, and supposing large parts of it of late origin (sometime in the second century), spun out fanciful theories about the "development" of the text we possess. But as Stephen Neill points out, "every serious scholar now agrees that the books were written not later than 100 A.D., that is, within seventy years of the death of Jesus Christ, and in the lifetime of at least some believers who had seen Him in the flesh." Most importantly, the Gospel of Mark "was written not more than forty years after the death of Christ," and "may have been written considerably

earlier." This dating is of immense importance. Whereas
the Tubingen school held that the gospel narrative had
evolved out of the life of the early Church, and reflected
not history but disputes within the early community (and
so "would have allowed us no more than the echoes of
early conflicts and tendencies in the primitive Church,
from which we could pick up faint gleams and shadows
of a real Jesus of Nazareth"), the earlier dating rules out
such an evolution. What disputes did occur took place
after the narrative was established.

The nineteenth-century conviction that the narrative
as we have it is all but worthless as history led a number
of writers to attempt "real" lives of Christ. Thus Renan
and Strauss produced so-called biographies of Jesus re-
flecting the naturalistic assumptions of their time and
interpreting all miracles as "myth." Strauss was trans-
lated by George Eliot; both were praised by Arnold;
both were widely read. A representative tragi-comic
Victorian figure emerged: Rose Macaulay's clergyman
who lost his faith as often as his collar-stud. But the
"myth" theory is also dead. Not only must the key documents be accorded an early date, but they were written
as history, by writers who knew what a historical fact is,
and to whom history was of supreme importance. According to modern scholarship, it "was of immense importance to the Christian that the later acts of God, like
the earlier [in the Old Testament], were acts of God in
history." Or again: "When the historian approaches the
Gospels, the first thing that strikes him is the extraordinary fidelity with which they have reproduced, not the
conditions of their own time, but the conditions of Palestine in the time and during the ministry of Christ."

Thus, if the older theory held that the Gospels had
evolved over an extended period, and that they were in
large part myths or fictions designed for the edification
of the early Christian community, we know that they
were of very early date, that the incidents they describe
were well known before they were written down, that in
the ethos of the community history was crucially important, and that a scrupulous regard was held for protecting
the narrative from accretion or distortion. Finally, we
know that the narrative was written down because the
community was turning outward to the world, and was

intended for people who did not know the living local tradition.[5]

As for the Resurrection story itself, which is absolutely decisive for Christianity, and for which the so-called biographies of Strauss, Renan and others had offered purely naturalistic explanations (thus moving, said Arnold, in the right direction), the best recent study is by Hans Freiherr von Campenhausen of the University of Heidelberg. In his *Tradition und Leben: Krafte der Kirchengeschichte* (1960) he includes a lengthy study of the Resurrection narratives. He attaches great weight to the historical evidence of I *Corinthians* 15, pointing out that the epistle was probably written in 56 A.D., less than thirty years after the Crucifixion, and that Paul, in touch with the leaders of the Church in Jerusalem, would hardly have confined his conversations with them to the issue of whether Gentiles should be taken into the Church. Von Campenhausen concludes that probably no more than ten years had passed between the Resurrection itself and the day on which Paul received first-hand information concerning the events of Christ's life from those who had direct knowledge of them. It is this knowledge that he claims to have transmitted to the Corinthians when he led them to Christ.[6] "It is only rarely," observes Stephen Neill, "that we have such good historical evidence for anything in the ancient world."

Plainly, this evidence cannot establish with finality the truth of the Resurrection story. But it is also fair at this point to ask the following question: supposing for a mo-

---

[5] As long as the preaching was in Palestine, where the events of the life and death of Jesus of Nazareth were widely familiar, little was needed beyond the *Kerygma*/the account of the Crucifixion and the Ressurection/. As soon, however, as missionary work moved out beyond these narrow limits to Caesarea and Antioch in Pisidia and Ephesus and Rome, almost of necessity the *Kerygma* of the Cross and Resurrection had to take a step backward in history, and to deal with the preaching of John the Baptist, and the ministry of Jesus.

[6] Here is the relevant passage in Knox's translation: "The chief message I handed on to you, as it was handed on to me, was that Christ, as the scriptures foretold, died for our sins; that he was buried, and then, as the scriptures foretold, rose again on the third day. That he was seen by Cephas, then by the eleven apostles, and afterward by more than five hundred of the brethren at once, most of whom are alive at this day, though some have gone to their rest. Then he was seen by James, then by all the apostles . . . and if Christ has not risen, then our preaching is groundless. Worse still, we are convicted of giving false testimony about God."

ment that the story *is* true, what *other* evidence than
what we do have might reasonably be expected?

We are driven to the conclusion, then, that the Gospels
are historical in intention. This is not to say, of course,
that they could not be mistaken or even deceitful, and
that is the question on which the whole issue turns.
Whether they are or not (through delusion or conspir-
acy) is precisely the question the individual judgment
must face, asking the question normally applied to any
testimony: number of witnesses, their agreement or lack
of it, their character and credibility (i.e. are they reliable
on other matters?), and so on. We will see how C. S.
Lewis' judgment operated here. But the Gospels are not
myth, and they are not mainly a reflection of Church
history. In this sense, sober modern scholarship leads
one to an attitude toward the Gospels which, oddly
enough, is closer to the traditional view of them—to the
view, say, of Dr. Johnson or Newman—than to that of
Strauss or Renan or Arnold.[7]

This is not to say for a moment, of course, that the
great critical effort of the nineteenth century, all the
science of Tubingen, was in vain. It possessed, to be
sure, perhaps more than its share of the pathos that so
often surrounds our enterprises. One thinks back on
Ferdinand Bauer (1792-1860), a heroic figure, tireless,
at his desk by four every morning, turning out in his
mature years 16,000 pages of scholarly prose—the
equivalent of a 400-page book every year for 40 years—
yet led by false assumptions "into error on every principle point of New Testament criticism." That there is
something ghastly about this does not need to be said.
And to the extent that scholarly error, eloquently dif-
fused by *literati,* helped to create a climate of opinion
dismissive on mistaken grounds of Christian claims, then
the critical movement must be said to have had tragic

---

[7] One would not guess from their paperback sales that the more recent
anti-historical approaches to the Gospels, those of Barth and Bultmann,
as well as of the so-called Form Critics, have been dealt with devastat-
ingly. See the relevant chapters in Neill, as well as *The Study of the
Synoptic Gospels* by Augustin Cardinal Bea (London, 1965). The attitude of both Barth and Bultmann has been conditioned by the tactics of
preaching: Bultmann wishes to give the narrative an existentialist meaning, and Barth deliberately turns away from the historical question in
order to purify and heighten the act of "faith." As for the Form Critics,
some of their basic axioms, upon which their whole approach depends,
have simply been shown to be false.

effects. Throughout the nineteenth century, indeed, the whole enterprise appeared baneful not only to the benighted but to men of sensitive conscience as well. Still, despite the fact that it made egregious mistakes and often created a misleading impression, we may see that through raising key questions the critical movement transformed the study of the Bible. Today we know more about the text, about the date and mode of its composition, about the meaning of key words and passages, and about the life of the early Church, than would have been possible without the critical movement. And if it has issued not in the destruction or demythologization of the Bible but in a strengthened sense of its value as historical evidence, then that is simply another of those ironies of which history is so fertile.

But this conclusion remains, I think it is fair to say, "specialized knowledge." It would not be known to the average professor of sociology or of English, let alone in the market-place. It is not known to Mr. Edmund Wilson.[8] Given this situation, C. S. Lewis, and before him G. K. Chesterton, had a vital and indeed unprecedented function to perform. They are, so to speak, *substitutes* for tradition. Until modern times, the majority of people received their knowledge of religious matters by a kind of cultural osmosis. Philosophical conclusions and doctrinal significance reached them through ceremony and sermon, custom and observance. They did not have to be scholars or reasoners to stand in some kind of relationship to specialized knowledge and to the insights of genius. But this condition no longer obtains. Not only does the life of the community no longer incorporate religious knowledge, but the churches themselves, in consequence of the cultural situation, too often have little intellectual vitality. I myself have heard only half a dozen sermons that were not outright insults to the intelligence of those who heard them. Indeed, a kind of historical reversal has taken place. At the beginning of the nineteenth century, the majority of people were Christians and were in a vital relationship with a con-

---

[8] When Wilson does venture into these areas, the results unfortunately are no better. His book on the Dead Sea Scrolls, published originally in the *New Yorker*, is a scandal to serious scholars, whatever their religious persuasion.

tinuous tradition. They actually knew a great deal about religious doctrine. If they did not always understand, they nevertheless read, the Bible. At the same time, a few advanced thinkers were skeptics. Today the masses, especially in the great cities, are quite cut off from tradition and know very little about Christianity even when they profess it. A great many are indifferent. The clergy seem more and more driven to making fantastic statements in order to attract attention, or perhaps through simple ignorance on their own part. But today, a number of advanced thinkers are Christians. The Victorian situation has been reversed. These circumstances define Lewis' role. "In the conditions produced by a century or so of Naturalism . . . we must get the truth ourselves or go without it."

For these tasks his mind had great virtues. He *knew* a great deal, in several senses of that word, but, in the most obvious sense of it, he was very learned. He was a classical scholar, and he knew both Latin and Greek, as well as several modern languages; he knew English literature over its whole range. He had had philosophical training: as we will see, his deviation into literature was a happy accident. We should never be mislead by the modesty of his tone or by the fact that he wears his learning so easily. He was a close, sentence by sentence student of the Bible, and of the Church Fathers; he knew theology and metaphysics. If, then, he functioned in his religious writings as a kind of surrogate for tradition, one cannot imagine a man better equipped to do so. C. S. Lewis *was* tradition—in perhaps the only mode in which it can really exist in our time.

A moment ago, I spoke of the "surprises" that constantly emerge in Lewis' writing. But I was far from meaning that he invents things, or that he introduces doctrinal novelty. No one could be less like the current Bishop of Woolwich or the current Bishop of San Francisco. In *The Screwtape Letters,* he notices the Vicar "who has been so long engaged in watering down the faith to make it easier for a hard-headed congregation that it is now he who shocks his parishioners with his unbelief, not vice versa." The point is worth stressing, and not only because of the comic Bishops of Woolwich and San Francisco. Only recently, the Dean of St. Paul's in London tacitly but unmistakably stated that the historicity of the Resurrection is neither here nor there, despite the fact that St. Paul had written: "if Christ has not risen, then our preaching is groundless. Worse still, we are convicted of giving false testimony about God."

X

Some years ago I happened to be attending a course of lectures on modern literature at a university in Boston. The lecturer was extremely good, he was devoted to modern literature, he was an atheist, and, not necessarily in consequence, he was far to the Left politically. As the weeks went by, he found himself increasingly embarrassed by the *Christianity* of so many of the writers he had to deal with, and whose works he loved. At long last he broke off the lecture and addressed the class personally and angrily. The class was made up of college students, for the most part Irish Roman Catholics from the Boston area. It was clear that he knew the writers in question better than anyone who was listening to him. "See here," he said, "these men, Eliot and Lewis and Tate and the others—*they* don't believe, what *you* believe: Heaven, Hell, the Virgin Birth, the Resurrection and all that. For *them* it's only a system of symbolism, a way of disciplining *feeling*."

No, it is not. Doctrinal differences aside—Lewis was an Anglican—and taking into account differences in erudition and intellectual power, Lewis believed precisely what those students believed, and in the same literal way. He knew what symbolism is, and he knew when symbolic language is being used, and he knew that men in the past had known this too; but he did not consider as symbolic the supernatural events of the Gospels, or the doctrines of the Virgin Birth and the Incarnation, and he did not think the doctrine of the afterlife a myth. The Bishop of California has recently announced that he has "given up" belief in the Virgin Birth. But Lewis, in his clear-minded way, knows what the issue really is, and he knows that the Advance of Science does not affect it one way or the other. We do know more about biology than St. Joseph did, but, on the point in question, he knew as well as we do the way in which infants ordinarily are conceived. He did not consider that what had happened was anything other than extraordinary. The real question at issue here is of presuppositions —i.e. is the universe the kind of place in which miracles can occur? The Spirit of the Age answers No, and many Liberal clergymen tacitly agree, even though, as Lewis says, if this is the case then "the claim which Christianity has been making for the last two thousand years is simply false." But in his very convincing book on the subject of miracles, Lewis faces the philosophical issue squarely, and answers Yes—on the evidence, the universe is that kind of place. Reflection can liberate one from a thoroughgoing naturalism. And while Lewis thought that "it is easier to argue, on historical grounds, that the Incarnation actually occurred than to show, on philosophical grounds, the probability of its occurrence," he also saw that the "historical difficulty of giving for the life, sayings and influence of Jesus any explanation that is not harder than the Christian, is very great. The discrepancy between the depth and sanity and (let me add) *shrewdness* of His moral teaching and the rampant megalomania which must lie behind His theological teaching unless He is God, has never been satisfactorily got over. Hence the non-Christian hypotheses succeed one another with the restless fertility of bewilderment." As for the Resurrection, some of the historical evidence for which we have touched upon a moment ago, Lewis believed that, far from being a myth, it had occurred, in history—in the same sense as, say, the Battle of Waterloo had occurred.

II
**CATHOLICS
AND PROTESTANTS
TODAY**

The Protestant
Deformation

HAROLD O. J. BROWN

Before the Great Ecumenical Movement, Protestant historians used to speak of the first few Christian centuries as the age of the formation of the Church. The Middle Ages then became the age of the deformation of the Church, to which a necessary remedy was prescribed: the Protestant Reformation. But if Luther and Calvin considered (not without cause, as the Roman-Catholic Counter-Reformation showed) the Christianity of the medieval church deformed, it is questionable whether they would consider the religion of their "Protestant" successors in the mid-twentieth century Christianity at all.

According to Protestant thought, the medieval church became deformed in the popular sense of the word when it no longer conformed to its essential principle of fidelity to a divinely revealed Word of God. But modern Protestantism is becoming deformed in the philosophical sense (losing its form [*forma*], its internal structural principle which gives it its distinctive character) because it is not merely out of conformity with the principle of fidelity to a divinely revealed Word of God, but it has surrendered it entirely, even rejected it on principle.*

Reacting to the Reformers' principle of *sola Scriptura*, the Roman Catholic Council of Trent defined the parallel authority of sacred tradition alongside Holy Scripture. For centuries the Protestant battle-cry against Roman Catholicism has been the charge that it elevates human teaching and traditions to the same level as divine revelation. The most devoted Catholic will admit that this charge has from time to time not been without some basis in fact, although he will seldom concede that the basis was sufficient to justify the Reformation. Whatever dangers there are in overemphasizing the value of tradition to the Christian church, the high regard for tradition within Roman Catholicism does mean that Roman Catholicism can continue to exist and function after a fashion even in the face of widespread ignorance of or disregard for the Scripture, because many of the basic teachings of the faith are also transmitted through the living tradition. Roman Catholicism without the Bible would be terribly impoverished, but to a certain extent it could survive without it, at least for a time. Since the sole authority of the Bible as the Word of God is Protestantism's basic formal principle, without Scripture Protestantism collapses like a punctured dirigible. Lacking a unified tradition, Protestantism without biblical authority is completely shapeless and purposeless, and inevitably takes its direction not from the teachings of the fathers (as Catholicism could still do in a similar extremity) but from the temper of the times.

Thus contemporary Protestantism is rapidly becoming characterized by two things: 1) the loss of its formal principle, which has for the past four hundred years given it its character and vitality, and 2) the substitution for this divine authority of whatever human authority is at the moment in fashion, without even the mediation of a generally accepted Christian tradition. Imagine a Protestant service in which the minister could, with a

---

* Very characteristically Bishop Robinson of Woolwich condemns traditional Christian ideas of right and wrong because they are derived "at second hand" from God (*Honest to God*, London, 1963, p. 106). That a Christian, and particularly a Protestant, could think that an idea was *inferior* because it was derived "second hand" from God shows how the concept of revelation has been rejected, and with it the very basic principle of Protestant Christianity, and in fact of all Christianity.

straight face, read from the pulpit Proverbs chapter 48 and the Hundred and Sixty-Ninth Psalm. He was reading from a notebook of favorite passages left him by a prominent member: apparently neither he nor the congregation noticed that the passages in question did not come from the Bible any more than the chapters cited actually exist in the books named. The service did not take place in some illiterate mountain village, but in Cambridge, Massachusetts. I have heard the following from the pulpit: "Our morning lesson is taken from C. P. Snow's *The Two Cultures.*" One hopes that these examples are not representative, but they are certainly not isolated. Clearly if Protestants do not know and read the Bible they cannot be guided and shaped by it. If not the Scripture, then what will give Protestantism its inner form?

Some theologians, such as Paul J. Tillich, have sought to substitute for the authority of biblical revelation the principle of non-conformity or of "protest" as the characteristic principle of Protestantism. This is based on the plausible but mistaken interpretation of the "protest" in Protestant: the first "Protestant," at the Protestation of Speyer in 1529, confessed and affirmed (*protestare,* to testify for) their loyalty and obedience to the Holy Scriptures. To substitute protesting in the modern sense of the word for this is to replace a positive principle with a negative and reactionary one. This is precisely what has happened, and modern Protestantism is becoming reactionary in the extreme: its only function consists in reacting negatively to its own biblical and doctrinal heritage in the theological sphere, and affirmatively to the currents of the time in the ethical sphere. It should also be noted in passing that the negative, reactionary principle of protest is a very poor basis for the continuing life of any church: it produces emergency and Ad Hoc committees overnight, but it cannot sustain the life of a community of faith through decades, much less through centuries.

Historic Protestantism and historic Roman Catholicism quarreled over what was to each an essential principle: the basis of authority. Protestantism placed it in obedience to the biblical revelation alone (*sola Scriptura*); Roman Catholicism urged the twin sources of Scripture and tradition.** Both agreed that there is a positive divine revelation, which must necessarily be obeyed despite what the world at large might say and do about it. This principle of obedience to God in opposition to the general opinion of mankind was behind the Roman government's charge that the early Christians were guilty of *odium humani generis*—hatred for the human race. Unfortunate as the Protestant-Catholic polemics of the sixteenth century were, they had this redeeming feature: they indicated the depth and fervor of the contenders' convictions. The ecumenical movement in the twentieth century is only in part due to an increase in mutual charity; in part it is also due to the feeling that there is no religious conviction important enough to quarrel over.

To the extent that it results from growing indifference, as distinguished from tolerance, the ecumenical movement is just as much a product of the modern secular mentality as the peace movement. The original pacifists were pacifists in obedience to what they took to be the will of God: for example, ordinary Christians in the second century, Anabaptists in the sixteenth. That they were not lacking in bravery was shown by their willingness to endure martyrdom at the hands of the government for their unwillingness to violate God's will as they understood it by taking up arms against the foreign aggressors. There is also a genuine humanist pacifism of the Schweitzer reverence-for-life school. But much of the modern ban-the-bomb variety of pacifism is not based on the principle that God forbids war, or that war is fundamentally destructive of human values, but rather on the negative conviction that there is no principle worth fighting or dying for.

Tolerance has always been a difficult virtue for adherents of the religions of the Book (Judaism, Christianity, Islam), while it has proved natural and easy for Hindus and Buddhists. It is difficult for a very good reason: all the religions of a specific divine revelation are based on a zeal for truth ("Thy Word *is* truth"). This very difficulty makes it a virtue. For Calvin and Cardinal

** This position, defined at the Council of Trent (1546-1563), seems to be being modified now. The question an orthodox Protestant must ask is: is the modification in the direction of elevating the authority of Scripture, or rather in the direction of denigrating the principle of divine authority ("Second hand"?) *per se?*

Sadolet to accept each other as in some sense Christian brothers, with each believing as passionately as he did in the truth of his own conviction, meant much more than it does today when a latitudinarian Protestant sits down with a Liberal Catholic. All too much Christian tolerance today is not based on the biblical principle of love, but upon the anti-biblical principle of indifference to questions of truth, and upon the feeling that right must always be found in compromise. Luther's "Here I stand!" is as out of date among Protestants as Leo X's "Anathema sit!" is among Roman Catholics, and to the extent that both have let them go out of date, they are in danger of disloyalty to the professed Lord, who claimed, "I am the truth." (*John* 14:6)

Thirty or forty years ago the struggle for the principle of biblical authority within Protestantism split Presbyterianism, America's most scholarly denomination, and others as well. Today unification of denominations is the cry, but it does not mean that differences have been resolved, but rather that they have been declared to be irrelevant. Here the churches are lining up with the worldly mentality of Pilate's time ("What is truth?" *John* 18:38), which is also the mentality of our own day, symbolized by Britain's greatest living philosopher affirming, "Better Red than dead." As an orthodox Protestant I can respect and love the Roman Catholic who opposes me much more than the Catholic Liberal whose attitude seems to be, "Really, now, we all believe in some sort of something, don't we?" But the "Catholic revolution" is still in progress; within Protestantism, the debacle is almost complete.

The success of the Protestant Deformation is shown by the fact that theological works in many quarters no longer dispute the principle of biblical authority. They either ridicule it as "second-hand," as John Robinson does, or ignore it, as Paul Tillich does. The latter's *Systematic Theology* makes virtually no use of the Bible as a source of religious knowledge; new books on Christian ethics quote from each other and from secular psychologists, but only rarely from Christ or the apostles. Protestant ignorance of the content and message of the Bible is becoming worse than that medieval ignorance which provoked Luther to his outbursts and Calvin to his

Institutes. Even the most obscurantist and ignorant medieval cleric would have agreed that one at least *ought* to know the Scriptures; for today's Protestantism, they are irrelevant. The medieval church at least had tradition, even if Luther's charges about its ignorance of the Bible are to be credited; modern Protestantism has no tradition, and thus without Scripture is cast entirely upon the values and goals of the surrounding world.

An almost total secularization of ethics is the other side of the deformation which results from the loss of the principle of authority. In consequence, Protestant ethics, like Protestant theology are coming to reflect nothing more than the mentality of the times. As late as the end of the First World War, American Protestantism was vigorous enough to throw itself into what it considered a religious crusade for prohibition *against* the temper of the secular world. Today's Protestantism has two major moral emphases: latitudinarian sexual ethics, and militant endeavor for civil rights. In contrast to the prohibition movement, neither of these results from a religious impulse. Apologists for sexual laxity in Christian moral teaching, like Joseph Fletcher of the Episcopal Theological School in Cambridge, Massachusetts, and John Robinson and Douglas Rhymes of the Diocese of Southwark in England, make it quite plain that their principal reason for wanting to revise Christian standards is that nobody likes them today. One might well ask whether anyone liked them in the Rome of St. Paul's time—but of course Paul's principle was not popularity with men, but fidelity to the will of God. If Jesus Christ had spared himself conflict with the mentality of His time, He could have spared himself the crucifixion.

Increasing Protestant interest in elections and legislation would look better if it could really be ascribed to religious motives. The present Protestant espousal of the civil rights movement, including many of its more dubious aspects, is no longer revolutionary, as abolitionism was before the Civil War. If American Protestants had espoused civil rights in the thirties, they might have claimed a religious motivation. But the flocking of clergy to the integrationists' banners today is nothing more than their participation, boosted by a few religious slogans, in a movement dictated by the mood of secular society. It is no more daring for a Massachusetts Baptist to espouse civil rights than it is for an Alabama Baptist to defend segregation; both positions could be of purely secular origin. It is significant that Protestant preachers proclaiming integration from their pulpits seldom do so on the basis of the teachings of Jesus Christ (although it is both possible and logical to do so), but prefer Gandhi or Myrdal as an authority. Thus a movement with Christian implications which could find support and guidance in Christian teaching is often in fact shown to be inspired and directed by the *Zeitgeist* rather than by the Holy Spirit.

The most apt commentary on the whole development can be given in the words of a recent meeting of campus chaplains at Harvard. The United Ministry at Harvard, having determined to publish an advertisement espousing the cause of civil rights, proposed as the keynote a quotation from James Baldwin's book, *The Fire Next Time*. Because Baldwin said, "Absolutely everything is in our hands," the Catholic priest objected, "Doesn't that leave God out?" This Protestant pointed out that Baldwin is outspokenly against Christian civilization, the Christian religion, and even the God of the Christians, and suggested that as clergy we would do much better to take our keynote from a biblical prophet of social justice like Amos. The Presbyterian chairman of the group answered the Catholic objection, "You're talking to Harvard and Radcliffe students. If you want them to listen you can't talk about God." To me he said, "Amos is dead. James Baldwin is alive." Motion carried, ad printed.

If Amos, and with him the other biblical writers, is dead in the minds of Protestant clergy, he will not lie alone for long: the whole Protestant church, deprived of its formative principle, will follow him into the grave. And this it is rapidly doing. Secularized Protestantism is celebrating its own funeral; Tillich and Robinson are declaiming the funeral orations, and the civil rights clerics performing the funeral dances. This is inevitable and probably desirable once the principle of authority has been lost. A secular church will not long survive. Yet even in the age of the Protestant deformation, as in the earlier medieval deformation, a spark is still preserved. Here and there, in small denominations, in individual churches, in small groups, the old principle of obedience to a divine revelation persists; where it does, there is still a church, and still a Lord. As Charles Malik stated, if the Christian faith has anything to it, the church will survive, to greet her Lord at His second coming, but many who thought that they were within her, while espousing the principles of the secular mind, will discover to their sorrow the truth of His words, "Not every one that saith unto me, Lord, Lord, shall enter into the Kingdom of Heaven, but he that doeth the will of my Father." (*Matthew* 7:21)

The Present Position
of Catholics

GARRY WILLS

Catholics are lucky to be living today. In fact, any student of Western religion must be enjoying this vivid moment of history. What seemed somewhat like a mausoleum, a short while ago, now looks somewhat like a madhouse.

It is a time of ferment—and of fizz. A time when impertinent bishops break into disorderly applause for a Patriarch who lets them know what is wrong with the Cardinalate—and when the same Patriarch is rapidly offered a Cardinal's hat, and takes it.

It is a time when Evelyn Waugh grumps that priests are only introducing the vernacular into the liturgy to prepare the way for the innovation they *really* want—permission for priests to marry; when a Maryland priest thinks using English in the Mass is a subtle way of attacking the Virgin Mary; when the Roman Curia labors manfully to protect its peculiar doctrine of the Pope's inerrancy from the errors of Pope John; when the Apostolic Delegate to America privately lets the bishops know that Rome did not really *mean* all it said about ecumenical services. A time, also, when the "freeing of the layman" is accomplished through a series of sermons telling Catholics to *submit* to the new liturgy (the bishops have spoken): when some priests patrol the aisles trying to shame their congregation into picking up the hymn books;

when the Pope advises preachers to have Catholics "give up Latin for Lent."

It is that time, too long deferred, when all Christians have begun to read the Bible together, and even translate it together; when seminarians of the various ministries study together, debating with fellow Christians, not with caricatured theses; when "the cloth" and "the collar" and some coifs formed a protective ring around the Negroes in Selma (a point that should perhaps be remembered when men propose the abandonment of clerical garb or nun's habits).

It is time when *Commonweal* editorial pages Made Their First Joke (of *course* you don't believe it, but look at the April 2, 1965, issue); when Catholics at last have a free and literate national newspaper; when the grammarless but monied editor of *Ramparts* acquires the rare distinction of marketing a tabloid at seventy-five cents a copy.

A time when a new American Cardinal is appointed and makes a stirring speech about the role of the press ("to disturb the comfortable"), and then, a month later, silences a silly priest because he kicks up a minor disturbance in the press. (The real scandal was the revelation that such an incoherent fellow could be professor of theology in a seminary.)

A time when *New Yorker* authors strive to live up to the maiden name of Father F. X. Murphy's mother (which happens to be Rynne;) when the authors of other "Council-books" try to live up to the *New Yorker;* when the Establishment gives its Good Housekeeping seal to the Papacy by means of a convocation called to honor an encyclical; when men who honor no other saints light journalistic candles to Pope John; when the *New York Times* decides it is safe, now, to take the Establishment's favorite Catholic in as religion editor.

A time when the Pope was reported to have given his tiara to the poor; only to have it turn out that he had given it to poor Cardinal Spellman (or to the poor nation of America, or the poor shrine in Washington, or Mr. Moses' poor Fair).

Pre-eminently a time of fads—when Teilhard de Chardin's publishers have a hard time spacing the appearance of his books on a market flooded with Teilhardiana; when

Catholics have come up with their own form of revivalism (called the "Cursillo"), in which "plants" strategically located among the participants get things holy-rolling, and the closing embraces sometimes get out of hand (a priest I know was lifted in the air and swung around twice).

A time when a Catholic editor suggests that the next Catholic "family of the year" be not such a crowd scene; when students threaten a scriptural "read-in" if the story of Susanna is "censored" from the English liturgy; when a priest, addressing a national gathering, updates the New Testament this way: "I was hungry and you supported the Alliance for Progress. I was thirsty and you worked to bring Peace Corps and Papal Volunteers to teach irrigation methods. I was sick and you wrote to your congressman about Medicare, and you perfected the Salk vaccine. . ."

A time when Dr. King calmly urges his people to love their oppressors in Selma, and a white editor of *Jesuit Missions* incites national hatred of them ("the worried, porcine face of Jim Clark was peering through the glass. Jim Clark, framed in a burial wreath. . . . For the Negroes, it was a moment delicious beyond words"). A time when the Catholic tradition on civil disobedience gets badly bent; when the Archbishop of Birmingham calls the mass beating of Negroes none of the nation's business but a local affair (undertaken, anyway, by men who are patriots); when the Archbishop of San Antonio calls Christ the great demonstrator.

It is a time of ecumenism, when the columnist Msgr. Conway proves that Catholics must stay out of the John Birch Society by observing that Robert Welch "proposes heresy" when he says religion is a subjective matter. Time when a diocesan paper, attacking a man's politics as racist, wanting to excommunicate him for *Something* but not quite daring (yet) to excommunicate him from the Church, says that he should be purged from—(Let's see, what *does* he belong to that we can publicly demand he resign from . . . Oh, yes!)—the Knights of Columbus.

It is a time when the Index, the Imprimatur, the secret Council, the canceled TV show, the suppressed report are happily fallen into disfavor, though not yet abolished; when it is hard to keep it silent that a silencing has taken place; when priests ask for a "bill of rights" in the conduct of theological condemnations; when men plead that the agony of those with a doubtful marital status be dealt with in terms of some other calendar than the millenial one used by ecclesiastical courts in Rome. It is also the time when California's Father DuBay wants to form a priest's union (going on strike, I suppose, by refusing absolution to us Catholic "employers").

A time when the "lay movement" is largely led by ex-seminarians who yearn, still, for a pulpit. When the Church's "triumphalism" is attacked by men who are triumphantly lyrical over their favorite theologians or their favorite (*i.e.*, their own) generation; when a book by 23 "young leaders" (See below, page 55) reveals, in a majority of cases, the simple pattern: Catholic boy goes to Harvard or Yale, comes back to find the old folks at home uninterested in Heidegger, and decides the old folks at home have been cheating him all his short life. Poor Oedipus (Poor mitred Laius!)

A time when daring spirits have to keep upping the ante to stay in. One will give you novenas and "Mari-olatry." Another throws in Cardinals and the Index. There go Catholic schools. Another tosses Hell away. The stakes get more interesting every day. The "sports" of yesterday are now conservatives.

And, through it all, a time of argument, of examination, of bucolic seminaries racked with sudden crises, of alliances, challenges, retreats, of new leaders, new voices, silly and sublime gestures, sacrifices, blunders. Who would miss it?

Time for all these things. And about time, too.

Some of the more intense objections to this ecclesiastical effervescence come, significantly, from non-Catholics. Many of those outside of the Church have been grateful to it for providing a point of stability in a giddy world. But those who live in a different ship and like to have a supplementary anchor can hardly complain if those who live entirely on that "anchor" try to make it a little more like a boat. An immobile Church *is* a useful component in an eclectic scheme; but bureaucratic introspection and paralysis are a constant drain on the integrity of those wholly committed to the Church.

Jesuit seminarians still read for a half hour every day

to "lay brothers" on the centuries-old assumption that the brothers are illiterate—though none are, anymore, in America. The attritive effect of living with a thousand little anachronisms of this sort, during formative years, has crippled the clerical leaders of the Church for too long a time. This ritualistic training easily leads either to resignation, a total surrender to routine, or to cynicism and resentment. In fact, the rather naive political Liberalism of many priests stems, I think, from a natural frustration with ecclesiastical "conservatism." There is often a serious lacuna in the priestly training, during which political awareness slumbers—to be awakened, as often as not, by fricton with repressive superiors. The Curia is anti-Communist and "conservative"; the relevant theologians are responsive to academic fashion, including the currents of modern Liberalism—that is all many priests know, when their political convictions "set"; and all (they think) they need to know.

This helps explain the fact that theological and political Liberalism so often come to men, now, as a "package," though there is more legal opposition than connection between the two. Theological Liberalism stands for the *total* tradition (scripture, the Fathers, the various Christian philosophies) over against a single, recent doctrine ("Thomism" in its "official" formulation over the last century). In matters of organization, it stands for decentralization, local variety "collegiality"; for a constitutional procedure in the workings of the Church's bureaucracy. In theology, it stands for the teacher over the administrator.

All of these matters have an obvious consonance with the concerns of present-day conservatism. It is the "consistent" Liberal in both fields who is faced with contradictions—a secular opposition to tradition and a theological emphasis on it; a desire to depose a central bureaucracy in Rome and enthrone one in Washington; a desire to break the uniformity of the seminary training and impose a monochromatic system on the public schools; a readiness for sweeping change and accumulating power in politics (without excessive scrupulosity over the Constitution's provisions), coupled with a desire for constitutionality as a protection from the Curia.

The thing conservatives should remember is that the present renewal is not a dissolution of the unchanging original Church, but the breakup of a temporal crust over the ancient vitality of the Faith.

The proof of this is the fact that scripture is at the heart of the renewal. The most important symbol of the Second Vatican Council was the enthroning of the Bible in its opening ceremonies. This has been obscured by attention to some externals—*e.g.*, by the desire to retain Latin (which some take to be a kind of eighth sacrament of the Church). The shift of habits is hard, and it has in many ways been mishandled; but the essential point in the liturgical changes is that they put the word of God back where it was in the early Church. The very criticism of new translations shows that people are thinking about the meaning of the sacred passages—something that few will claim took place in the Latin Mass. (Devotees of the Latin should recall what a hard time St. Jerome had get-

ting his great translation accepted into the liturgy they now elegize. Even St. Augustine opposed the changes, and certain parts of the Psalms never did give way to Jerome's superior rendering.)

As in all times of change, there have been excesses—but surprisingly few. The gloomy predictions Church "conservatives" might have made some years ago—of heresy, schism, irresponsible individualism, crises of authority, defection of priests, anti-clericalism — have no actual evils to fasten on. At a time when the press, hungry for religious news, exaggerates the slightest conflicts (like the shadowy "Traditionalist Movement," a head without a body—and not much of head at that), there have been no doctrinal aberrations, no movements toward disobedience. The reforms are sometimes over-celebrated, or praised for the wrong reasons; but the leaders of the reform are sound theologians, acting *with* the bishops and the Council not against them. It would be blind prejudice to describe what is going on as the result of a "fever for change," or to oppose it out of an undiscriminating preference for the past. The question is: *Which* past? That of St. Thomas, or of nineteenth-century Thomists? That of St. Augustine, or of a thin puritan residue of Calvinized Augustinianism? That is a *conservative* reform, and perfectly fits Johnson's definition of conservation: "The act of preserving; care to keep from perishing; continuance; protection."

I am not making a plea for blanket approval of the new tendencies in the Church. In fact, when I said that this is an exhilirating time to be alive, I realized the statement would not apply to doctrinaires on either side. They are not enjoying it at all. Evelyn Waugh, that great man and great stylist, languishes pre-Raphaelitically, longing for the Mass that (as he said) allowed his mind repose. He has earned his repose—though many others who take his position have not. On the other side, the doctrinaire Liberals are no happier for seeing the changes they wanted now take place. If anything, the wilder ones seem less satisfied than ever. That group also contains estimable men; but neither extreme, however discerning in other matters, is sensitive to the vital impulses shaping Catholic change in this century: A more discriminating response is needed for that. The key biblical text for the times should be the one that describes the wise steward (*i.e.*, the household *conservator*) as bringing forth from his storeroom things new and old.

III
THE CHRISTIAN
IN THE
MODERN WORLD

Conservatism, Liberalism and Religion

WILL HERBERG

It can reasonably be contended that one of the most revealing characteristics of conservatism and Liberalism as political philosophies is their radically different attitudes toward religion. For religion in some sense is the most significant thing about a culture; and even in so-called "secular" societies it is very often a profound and illuminating touchstone of cultural attitudes.

Liberalism, some one has acutely observed, is Jacobinism *sans guillotine*. It exhibits the same urge to incessant innovation, the same infatuation with human reason, the same penchant for rationalistic blueprints along which to "new-model" the body politic, the same confidence in the omnipresent, omnicompetent State. The Liberal, however, is frightened at the violence and terror of Jacobinism; he hopes to accomplish Jacobin ends without Jacobin means, to make the omelette (as the true-blue Jacobin tauntingly reminds him) without breaking the eggs.

At no point, perhaps, is the inner bond between liberalism and Jacobinism so obvious as in their common hostility to religion in public life, and in their common commitment to the thoroughly secularized laic state. In the original Jacobin creed, religion was held to be the

primal superstition corrupting the innate rationality of
"the man and the citizen," and the Church was that "In-
famous Thing" which had to be "wiped out" if men were
ever to be free. This radically secularistic logic of Jacobinism took some time to reveal itself because many of the
early Jacobins were still infected with eighteenth-century
Deism and saw themselves replacing the traditional religion of the people with the "pure Cult of the Supreme
Being." But already in the course of the French Revolution, Robespierrean Deism had to face the atheistic
"Cult of Reason," promoted by Hebert, Chaumette, and
the *enrages*. Later Jacobinism was fiercely anti-religious,
determined to extirpate religion not only from public
life. The Liberals, by and large, shared this bias, but
pressed their campaign in their own "Liberal" way. Religion, they insisted, was to be a "private matter," a
matter of personal taste; the "modern state," on the
other hand, was to be raised on purely secular foundations. The state, in short, was to be "religion-free" and
"religion-blind," refusing so much as to recognize the
existence of religion as a public concern. But since no
enduring social order is possible without some common
set of ideas, values, and purposes, the "religion-free"
Liberal State necessarily came to mean a state in which
the pseudo-religion of secularism was enthroned and established in irreconcilable conflict with the traditional
religions of the West. To have seen this so clearly consti-
tutes the great merit of the so-called "reactionary" papal
encyclicals of the nineteenth century, however open to
criticism these encyclicals may be on other grounds. Liberalism insisted on the extrusion of religion from public
life so that the void could be filled with the secularistic
gospel of Liberalism itself.

The Liberal program, often championed by the most
tolerant, most high-minded of men (such as John Stuart
Mill), came to fruition in the brutal anti-clerical, anti-
religious legislation of the French Radical Socialist
(bourgeois radical) regimes in the early part of this century. Every effort was made, by the power of the law,
to confine the priest to sacristy or cloister, to wipe out
religious schools, and to forbid religious orders from engaging in education, or even to have a legal existence on
French soil. The State was to be the only educator (*l'Etat*

enseignant), the only power entitled to influence the people or form the mind of the rising generation. "There are no rights but the rights of the State," declared Emile Combes, premier from 1902 to 1905, and a prime mover of the anti-religious legislation. "There is no authority but the authority of the Republic." Never has the totalistic logic of secularistic Liberalism been so openly proclaimed and so clearly revealed as in these words of the enlightened Liberal statesman.

Lenin and the Bolsheviks, who, personally and as a party, were committed to the total extirpation of religion, operated with the same logic when they took power in Russia in November 1917. The first decree on religion, issued by the new regime shortly after the coup d'etat, declared religion to be a "private matter," and took measures for expelling it from the public realm, which was to be the monopoly of the new Party-State. Very much the same provision has been continued in every Soviet constitution since.

Conservatism, on the other hand, has always found in religion—the traditional religion of the community—both the basis and the pinnacle of the culture and, while not denying its true inwardness, has seen it primarily in its public aspect. Conservative thinkers, from Edmund Burke to Russell Kirk, have believed and proclaimed that, without religion, the body could not survive as a moral entity. Religion, conservatives have agreed, is the spring of social coherence and civic virtue; it binds the community together, it hallows custom, and softens the harsh outlines of power; it humanizes man and so stabilizes society. Perhaps no one has reflected more deeply on the role of religion in modern political society than Alexis de Tocqueville, who saw with foreboding the rise of democratic mass society and felt that nothing could tame this awakening giant and prevent him from destroying all freedom and culture except the civilizing force of religion. He agreed with George Washington that "reason and experience both forbid us to expect that national morality could prevail in exclusion of religious principle," and stressed that democracies depend upon religion, since "liberty cannot be established without morality, nor morality without religion."

For Tocqueville, the realistic aristocrat confronted

with mass democracy, religion was a conservative, one might almost say preservative, force; and so it has remained in conservative thinking since. Apart from private devotion, religion is prized primarily as a spiritual "inner check," curbing, mollifying, and thereby also integrating in the invisible way in which true societies are integrated. Whether religion is to be officially established or not, and in what way, are matters of prudence and historical circumstance. What is fundamental in conservative conviction is that religion is of public concern and properly belongs in the realm of public life. For, as the celebrated Article 3 of the Northwest Ordinance of 1787 puts it: "Religion, morality, and knowledge [are] necessary to good government and the happiness of mankind. . . ."

There is obviously a great deal of wisdom in the conservative understanding of religion as a spiritual force of integration, and we have never been in such need of this wisdom as we are today. Yet it is impossible for the man of faith not to feel uncomfortable with religion so understood. The man of faith feels that somehow, if so understood, religion is not taken with ultimate seriousness. I have quoted some words from Washington's Farewell Address. Let me quote the whole passage:

> *Whatever may be conceded to the influence of refined education on minds of peculiar structure, reason and experience both forbid us to expect that national morality can prevail in exclusion of religious principle.*

Here George Washington, the sincere Christian, is all but admitting—so much the man of the eighteenth century is he—that for enlightened minds which have enjoyed the benefits of a "refined education," religion may, after all, perhaps not be so necessary! When religion is thus conceived and valued instrumentally, some such suspicion is inevitable.

Religion—certainly the biblical religion informing Judaism and Christianity—is deeply rooted in tradition; indeed, it is itself the main vehicle of the historical continuity of tradition upon which every living society must ultimately depend. And yet religion—most emphatically the biblical religion informing Judaism and Christianity

—can never accept the role that the conservative, in his eagerness to conserve what is indeed worth conserving, assigns to it. Religion sanctions society, but cannot become simply its handmaiden; it sustains the social order, but at the same time subjects it to a radical, and what must sometimes seem a shattering, criticism. Its standpoint cannot be simply that of society itself; it cannot let itself be robbed of its transcendence without letting itself be converted into an idolatrous cult sanctifying every social order simply because it is the social order that happens to prevail. Our religion, after all, is the religion of Amos, Isaiah, Jesus, and Paul, who certainly did not conceive of the word of God as simply a stabilizing, society-sustaining force.

The conservative's dilemma at this point is a real one. He affirms religion as the moral foundation of civil society; but *unless he is something more than a conservative*, he will be tempted to turn religion into an exalted public utility serving social and cultural ends; and this true religion will not tolerate. The prophetic faith of the Bible is not a faith that can be domesticated or contained in simply conservative categories. If the secularistic Liberal is always trying to expel religion from the com-

"I'm an atheist, too, but I'm afraid I'm not very devout about it."

mon life, the secular-minded conservative is forever
tempted to make of it a mere instrument of social order.
The man of faith must protest against both. And a conservatism conscious of its own nature and limits will
surely recognize the legitimacy and necessity of this religious protest.

Religious Instruction: A Natural Right

RUSSELL KIRK

Edmund Burke declared that one of the most important *real* natural rights was the right to instruction in life—along with the right to consolation in death. He meant primarily *religious* instruction, of which the French revolutionaries were depriving the French nation.

Christianity and Judaism in America will not be overthrown by violence; but the whole religious foundation of our civil social order may be undone by a doctrinaire league of our omniscient Supreme Court with the arrogant secularism of certain educationists. Two recent books make it clear how real this peril has become.

One of these books is *To Pray or Not to Pray*, by Charles Wesley Lowry (The University Press of Washington, D.C., student edition, $2.75). Dr. Lowry is the head of the respected Foundation for Religious Action in the Civil and Social order (Dupont Circle Building, Washington, D.C.), a tax-exempt association which costs only a few dollars a year to join, and which I commend heartily to all readers of this page.

The other book is *The Messianic Character of American Education*, by Mr. Rousas J. Rushdoony (Presbyterian and Reformed Publishing Company, Philadelphia,

$6.50). Mr. Rushdoony, a Calvinist clergyman and scholar, holds a higher degree in education.

To Pray or Not to Pray is a "handbook for study of recent Supreme Court Decisions and American Church-State Doctrine" and extremely useful. Dr. Lowry, an Episcopalian, the author of the well-known *Communion and Christ*, demonstrates through documents that there is no sound basis for the notion (though it is entertained by the Supreme Court today) that the first clause of the First Amendments prevents religious instruction in public schools. Interference with such instruction is not only unpopular; it is bad law, in which conclusion Dr. Lowry is reinforced by Dean Edwin R. Griswold and other authorities. As Mr. Lowry sees the Court decisions which give arrogant secularism a monopoly of public schools:

> *Can it be said that what has happened is the result of changing public opinion and is therefore a true expression of American democracy? The answer would seem to be clearly in the negative. All the evidence is that the overwhelming majority of our people accepted and approved the practices that have been struck down. Once again it is the Supreme Court that is ahead of the people and seeks to direct them, not in accordance with legal precedents but in obedience to current philosophical judgments. Opinion in the Court is, of course, not isolated. It exists among elite groups in the country as a whole and is expressive of an ideology that has been gaining adherents among American intellectuals. It has, however, picked up real speed only in the last generations. It is an ideology and its name is secular Liberalism.*

The Messianic Character of American Education traces systematically the development, among educationists, of an anti-religious bigotry which seeks to supplant Christian and Judaic faith and learning by a muddy "religion of democracy"—the ideology to which Dr. Lowry refers. Mr. Rushdoony discusses Horace Mann, James G. Carter, Edward A. Sheldon, Henry Barnard, William Torrey

Harris, John Swett, Charles de Garmo, Francis Wayland Parker, William James, Nicholas Murray Butler, G. Stan-

ley Hall, Herman Harrell Horne, John Dewey, J. B. Watson, Carleton Washburne, Edward Lee Thorndike, Boyd H. Bode, William Heard Kilpatrick, Harold O. Rugg, George S. Counts, and Theodore Brameld—who, differing among themselves though they do, all have contributed to the secularizing of American schools.

"It is self-evident that on this scheme," Mr. Rushdoony concludes, "if it is consistently and persistently carried out in all parts of the country, the United States system of national popular education will be the most efficient and wide instrument for the propagation of Atheism which the world has ever seen." Mr. Rushdoony is referring immediately to the lectures of A. A. Hodge, in 1887, warning Americans against "the supremacy of the lowest common denominator"; but Supreme Court decisions and the concentration of power in an educational bureaucracy now make it possible, unfortunately all too possible, to realize Hodge's grim prediction.

All schooling originated as religious instruction. If the whole religious foundation of education is demolished, the elaborate edifice of American public instruction cannot stand. Teachers must answer questions concerning the first principles of human nature, of the sciences, and of social order; and if they are forbidden to give religious answers, then they must give anti-religious answers—or else remain silent on the first concerns of the rising generation.

So in the name of the "rights" of a tiny minority of militant atheists and secularists, the American people are denied the fundamental natural right of religious instruction. True, they may seek it in Sunday schools; but an hour on Sunday has no chance against twenty-five hours or more of anti-religious state instruction the rest of the week.

Either such instruction is made constitutional again—through amendment or through the Supreme Court's reversing itself—or else we are going to have "bootleg" religious instruction in the public schools; for already many school districts are defying the Court's absurd decisions. The American people do not intend to be deprived of the most fundamental sort of knowledge.

The Christian
Social Sentimentalist

E. v. KUEHNELT-LEDDIHN

What are the deeper reasons for the ever mounting fascination with "social justice," today prevalent among Christians in general and Catholics in particular? Why the *apertura a sinistra*, and the worker-priest experiment? Professor Wilhelm Roepke once stated emphatically that nothing is more dangerous than to discuss economics without regard for ethical considerations, or to moralize in economics without being conversant with the realities of economic life. In the last two hundred years of Western history the sentimentalists crusading for some sort of "justice" or to "right the balance" have caused more tears and bloodshed than the simple, egotistic materialists who merely crave for earthly goods.

Christianity most obviously is concerned with moral values and ethical attitudes. In medieval scholastic theology love of one's neighbor was the highest of all virtues, therefore the works of charity were encouraged by the medieval Church. When Luther condemned *Werkheiligkeit* (sanctification by good works) the drive for charitable action slackened—but not permanently. In modern times the Reformed Faiths have been almost as much engaged in charitable works as the Catholic Church. . . and in some countries even more so.

A certain affection for the poor has always been in the Christian tradition. Christ said that the poor would always be with us and he warned that material ties could endanger the spiritual welfare of the rich, whose entry into Heaven was as difficult as the passing of a rope (*kamilos,* not *kamelos*) through the eye of a needle. There arose, moreover, the myth of Christ the pauper, the indigent son of a humble carpenter. *Tekhnon,* however, also means architect or building contractor. Joseph was a landowner in the Bethlehem region and when the Magi arrived he already had a house; in addition, he was of royal blood ("Son of David!") which made Jesus a pretender to the throne and created endless misunderstandings between Him and His people. The Virgin Mary was the niece or grandniece of St. Elizabeth who belonged to the highest social layer. The "proletarian myth" about the Savior helped to present Him as a social reformer—which He never was. In more than one sense He was the King of Kings. Nor did He preach only to "simple fishermen"— if St. John the Evangelist wasn't a first-rate intellectual, who is?

In our days theologians have become concerned with the problem of "social justice" which by no means identical with charity. The impetus in modern times to establish "social justice" came undeniably from the Marxists who condemned the inequalities of wealth, insisting that political equality must be supplemented by economic equality. Yet this clearly meant a break with the Christian tradition which embraced Ulpian's *suum cuique,* "to everybody his own." The Christian tradition accepts, at best, "adverbial equality" (to "have equally") but not essential equality (to "be equal"). According to Christian doctrine we are certainly not equal even "in the eyes of God." Judas Iscariot expiring in the noose and St. John dying in Patmos were not "equal before God"; there is no equality of Grace, no equality in Heaven, none on Earth, none in Purgatory, none in Hell (although one might say that in a deeper sense, equality *is* Hell).

Socialism, from St. Simon and Engels to Lenin and Trotsky, became a movement of intellectuals (mostly of bourgeois and upper crust origin), calculated and designed to mobilize the envy of the economically less fortunate masses. The reason for the masses' unsatisfactory material status was assumed by the Socialists to be "exploitation" or other obstacles put in their way by the "rich." But frequently there were other reasons too: natural catastrophies, ignorance or laziness.

These remarks by no means invalidate the *possibility* of a socially unjust order. The Catholic Church awoke to the existence of such a problem at the end of the nineteenth century. The Encyclical *Rerum Novarum* of Leo XIII dealt with it closely. Forty years later, in the Encyclical *Quadragesimo Anno,* Pius XI (with the aid of Father Gustav Gundlach S.J. of the Gregorian University) again approached the problem. And more recently, the Encyclical *Mater et Magistra,* signed by Pope John XXIII and elaborated by professors of the newly created Lateran University, enjoying the special protection of Cardinal Ottaviani, has once more taken up the theme. Needless to say, these Encyclicals talk in general terms, never referring to specific areas, countries, or enterprises. And it is certainly consistent with the spirit of Catholic theology that the Church is concerned with the problem of justice in the economic domain. Still, when it comes to the practical application of the Encyclicals, the individual Catholic is entirely on his own, and in concrete cases he can only pass moral judgment or suggest "reforms" if he is in the possession of all the facts.

If we ask ourselves where, *in concreto* in the free world, economies based on actual large-scale exploitation exist, we will be hard pressed to find such areas. The Church's moralizing injunctions have created a probably unforseen sense of illusion among good Christians who are not necessarily swept off their feet by the general tidal waves of jealousy but actually become unthinking victims of visual impressions. Obviously there are considerable differences in wealth and income even in "progressive democracies" like Sweden, Switzerland, or the Netherlands. Even more obviously there is a terrifying discrepancy between the very rich and the very poor in "backward" nations where poverty, if not misery, is prevalent. But in the case of each country we have to collect the data pertaining to national wealth, national gross income, wages, salaries, investment rates and profits. And before we can arrive at a rational judgment, before we can demand "social reforms" and a more rigorous application of social principles as set down in the Encyclicals or other Christian documents, we must know the exact score.

Christian social sentimentalism is greatly responsible for the steady growth of Italian Communist votes (without a parallel rise in Communist conviction, we might add). Since the workers' wages have increased in Italy by leaps and bounds while more and more Communists were being seated in Parliament, the little Italian has had the impression that this was due to a greater liberality on the part of the entrepreneurs, caused by fear of the Communists; hence it is considered wise to increase this fear. But to believe that the Italian employer is more generous to his employees because he trembles before the Communist menace (or because he reads the social Encyclicals of the Popes) is nonsense; he pays maximal wages *anyhow*. The truth is that the gross national product is much bigger, and that, thanks to wise investment, good management, and greater trade volume, the output per manhour has grown considerably (until recently).

But before we mention other countries or nations let us face the grim fact that what we call the standard of living compatible with the "dignity of man" is of most recent attainment. Only the combination of sustained hard work, technology, rationalization and organization, savings, and sound investments could achieve the miracle of a fairly general affluence—a miracle which has only taken place in recent times and only in the Western world. The flair for objective reality (the engineer was born in the shadow of the Cross and of Aristotelian realism!) and personal ambition were essentials. Our medieval forefathers, needless to say, worked very little. A hundred holidays besides the 52 Sundays were the norm in Central Europe. The puritanical spirit of the Reformation and the invention of labor-saving devices (which are expensive and cannot be left idling) sped up a rhythm of work unknown in Africa or South Asia. Hence the West (Europe and America) left the older cultures of Asia and Africa way behind.

The dream of a substantial increase of lower class incomes or of welfare through "social engineering," confiscatory taxation, or other feats of "social justice" is baseless. The re-distribution of wealth never stretches far enough for more than a trivial alleviation of poverty, and redistribution can be used but once, at that.

Finally, there is the terrible fear that the Christian Churches may miss the boat, a fear sustained by the conviction that we as Christians "have to take the wind out of the sails of Socialism and Communism—by aping some of their policies." This purely strategical-tactical (and utterly un-Christian) trend of thought is strengthened by the widespread notion that "in the past" the Church "always sided with the rich." The Church, naturally, usually condemned Marxism and materialism but one truly wonders when and where she is supposed to have espoused the cause of the Rich. This legend has to be looked into carefully—just as the legend of the "rich Church" in our times. (I would like to know in which solidly Catholic country the majority of priests attain materially a middle-class level!)

Of course, envy is an ugly vice and a leading Catholic theologian explained to me that even if no benefit accrues to the lower classes, the wealth of the rich should be partly expropriated just because it generates so much envy and jealousy. I asked him what he would do, for instance, in the case of two sisters, one beautiful and one ugly. The ugly one is jealous and bursting with envy. Should one disfigure the beautiful sister merely so as not to lead the other into temptation—or should one preach virtue to her? He had no answer.

I have asked another theologian of renown (an Austrian), who is at the same time an eminent economist, whether a young man who inherits ten million dollars and builds castles and palaces with this sum would not actually perform a social service. The theologian was hesitant. Up to a point I was right, he said, but the turn-over of the money would be very slow. Invested in indus-trial enterprises it would better serve the common good. I suggested museums and libraries instead of palaces and castles. The answer was the same, naturally. But what if the nauseating young man were to buy 1,000 racing cars of different colors? The theologian-economist smiled sadly. Yes, I had him there.

Yet, the Christian social sentimentalist does not aban-don his sometimes truly dangerous dreams and his com-pletely bona fide, occasionally even unselfish, dema-goguery. At the Vienna *Katholikentag* in 1952 Pius XII insisted that a proletariat existed almost nowhere in Europe today except in our Mediterranean "deep South," but the trembling fear that the Church might be accused of a reactionary behavior and mentality still elicits shrill demands for "social changes."

A Religious 'Right' to Violate the Law?

WILL HERBERG

In 1965, Yale University conferred the degree LL.D. upon Martin Luther King, who had already been celebrated on the cover of *Time* Magazine. True enough, nowadays the LL.D., *legum doctor,* doctor of laws (both canon and civil), no longer implies any special distinction in jurisprudence or legal learning; but it does imply a moral and social distinction which sets off its recipient as a man of intelligence, eminence, and respectability, a force in society and a leader of men—and this Dr. Martin Luther King certainly is. Dr. King is also a Christian, and sees the movement he leads as a Christian movement, grounded in Christian teachings.

It is therefore of considerable interest to inquire a little more closely into Dr. King's notions of political responsibility and social order, particularly into his central contention that Christian principles permit, perhaps even require, the violation of laws the individual conscience may hold to be "unjust." In this contention Dr. King is supported by that other influential Negro Christian leader, the Rev. Adam Clayton Powell, who is also a member of the House of Representatives. Here are their words:

> *Dr. Martin Luther King*: "One may well ask, 'How can you advocate breaking some laws and obeying others?' The answer lies in the fact that there are two types of laws: There are *just* laws and there are *unjust* laws. . . . I submit that an individual who breaks a law that con-

science tells him is unjust, and willingly accepts the
penalty. . . is in reality expressing the highest respect
for law . . ." ("A Letter From the Birmingham City
Jail").

Rev. Adam Clayton Powell: "People say it's against
the law. What law? And who made them? There is
only one great and unbreakable law, and that's the law
of God" (recorded Feb. 4, 1964 by NBC-WRC News).

The two are in substantial agreement (Dr. King too
derives "just" laws from "the moral law or the law of
God"); and, in more or less cautious form, their position
is shared by thousands of churchmen, Negro and white,
throughout the country. But how does this position square
with well-established Christian teaching on government,
law, and civil obedience?

The essential Christian teaching on government, law,
and civil obedience is grounded on that celebrated Chapter XIII of Paul's Epistle to the Romans, which itself
reflects earlier Jewish teaching. "Let every one be subject
to the governing authorities," the Apostle enjoins. "For
there is no authority except from God, and the existing
authorities have been ordained by God. Therefore, he
who resists the authorities resists what God has appointed,
and those who resist will incur judgment. . . ." This is
balanced in the New Testament by the conviction of
Peter and the Apostles, "We must obey God rather than
man" (Acts 5:29).

When does loyalty to God come into conflict with
obedience to earthly rulers? When earthly rulers are
insensate enough (as totalitarian states invariably are)
to demand for themselves what is owing only to God—
worship and ultimate allegiance. The classical Christian
teaching emerges most profoundly perhaps in the writings
of St. Augustine, whose position Professor Deane thus
summarizes:

> All the laws promulgated by the ruler must be
> obeyed by all citizens, with the sole exception of laws
> or commands that run contrary to God's ordinances . . .
> When Augustine says that God's command over-
> rules [human] laws and customs, it seems clear that he
> is referring to those commands of God that have been
> directly revealed to men in the Scriptures, such as the
> prohibition against idol-worship . . . He does *not* say
> that if the ruler is unwise or evil, and fails to take the

eternal law into account when he frames temporal laws, these laws have no validity, and the subjects have no obligation to obey them; nor does he say that the subjects have a right to determine for themselves, by reference to the natural or eternal law, whether or not such a temporal law is valid and is to be obeyed" (Herbert A. Deane, *The Political and Social Ideas of St. Augustine*, Columbia U.P., 1963, pp. 147, 89, 90; Dr. Deane is professor of government at Columbia).

This, in substance, early became the normative Christian doctrine, stated and restated by Thomas Aquinas, Martin Luther, John Calvin, and every other great moralist and theologian of the Church. It is the standard by which the position advanced by Dr. King and Rep. Powell *as Christian* must be judged; and, judged by that standard, their position permitting the violation of any law disapproved of by the individual conscience as "unjust," must be judged as not Christian at all, but seriously deviant and heretical.

The early Christians, under the teaching of the apostles, were enjoined to obey the laws of the state, a pagan state, mind you, whether they held these laws to be just or unjust—just so long as the state (the Emperor) did not claim for itself the worship and allegiance owing only to God. At that point, they knew how to draw the line. But even at that point, where they were compelled to disobey, their disobedience was limited to *refusal to participate* in the pagan abominations. The Christian refused, at the risk of life, to take part in the pagan cult, or to sacrifice to the Emperor; he did not set up mass picketing of the temples, or organize sit-ins in the public buildings in which the "blasphemies" (Tertullian) were being performed. Dr. King will get as little support for his position from authoritative Christian practice as from authoritative Christian teaching.

Would it not be well for Dr. King as a responsible community leader honored with a Doctor of Laws by Yale University, to consider the consequences of his strange doctrine? Every man has his conscience; and if the individual conscience is absolutized (that is, divinized), and made the final judge of laws to be obeyed or disobeyed, nothing but anarchy and the dissolution of the very fabric of government would result. Thousands and thousands of Americans, eminent, respectable, and responsible, are convinced in their conscience that the new Civil Rights Act is utterly wrong, unjust, and unconstitutional; are they therefore entitled to disobey it, and to organize civil disobedience campaigns to impede its effectuation? Grant this "right" and there would be no law at all, nothing but a clash of "consciences" that could not hope to escape becoming a clash of raw power.[1] Strange as it may seem to Dr. King, the very purpose of government is to make us obey laws of which we do *not* approve, which indeed we may even regard as "unjust." Laws that we approve of, and regard as just, we hardly need much coercion to get us to obey.

In its essential aims, the civil rights movement led by Dr. King is not at all revolutionary: it strives not to subvert and new-model the American system, but to win for the Negro a fair and equal place within it. Its methods, however, and the political philosophy that informs these methods—the deliberate creation of "crisis-packed situations" through systematic civil disobedience—are consistent neither with Christian teaching nor with ordinary political responsibility.[2] Dr. King, the Christian leader, now a Yale Doctor of Laws, might do well to rethink the theological foundations of a doctrine so dubious in its social and political consequences.

---

1. One important exception must be noted. Under the American system of judicial review, the constitutionality, and therefore the legality, of a law, when challenged, cannot be finally determined until it comes to court; and, very frequently, it cannot come to court until it is somehow violated. Such technical violation for the sake of a *test case* is to be fundamentally distinguished from the mass civil disobedience advocated by Dr. King.

2. The pitch of irresponsibility this kind of thing can lead to is painfully illustrated by the words addressed by that eminently respectable citizen, Adlai E. Stevenson, to the graduating class of Colby College in Maine: "I think especially of the participation of American students in the great struggle to advance civil and human rights in America. Indeed, even a jail sentence is no longer a dishonor, but a proud achievement. Perhaps we are destined to see in this law-loving land people running for office not on their stainless record, but on their prison records."

The Third Eye

FREDERICK D. WILHELMSEN

I take my title from the last line of the afterword, written by John Cogley, to this collection of essays by twenty-two younger Catholic intellectuals. If there *is* a Third Eye fitted into the ocular equipment of these men, it is a colossal tear jerker. I have never in my life read so much downright whining in any other 245 pages pressed together to make a book. This generation may go with a bang but it has certainly come in with a whimper. The writers among them complain about bad reviews. The teachers complain about repressive university administrations. Almost everybody beats the poor parish priest over the head and absolutely nobody has a good word for the Knights of Columbus or the Holy Name Society. The rank and file laity, those big shot slobs who never heard of Teilhard de Chardin and who could not care less about the *mystique* of the Dialogue, get a big bad time for their indifference to liturgical reform and for their residual conservatism. Favorite targets are Goldwater, *National Review*, Madame Nhu and Cardinal Ottaviani.

But let the text speak for itself: it is loaded with good things. We encounter an inferiority complex, as in Curley's "those of us who teach and administrate, create and criticize, should not have less respect for man than does a Marxist humanist." We come up against philosophies which deny the Christian structure of American society, as in strictures against "the Catholic uproar over the present school prayer ruling" (Ahearn). We suffer childish arrogance reminiscent of Plato's unjust man, the man who meddles in affairs not his own, in statements about

"the utterly deficient parishes that I knew in New York,
Providence, and New Haven (you guessed it, you de-
ficient pastors in New York, Providence, and New
Haven! Ahearn once again!).

We face the conviction that every opening-to-the-left is
beneficial but that any gestures towards the right are
evil, as in the report that "good things happened at Catholic University . . . one could go well to the left . . . and
I did" (John F. Bannan). We yawn over *pronunciamen-
tos* against "the official Church and clerical intransig-
ence" (friend Bannan). We are amused by the old fairy
tale as to "why should it have taken two hundred years
for the Church to recognize the mistake it made with
Galileo" (Douglas Cole). We are warned with due
solemnity against the mentality that responds to "Lourdes,
indulgences, Index, Ottaviani, relics, . . . McCarthy,
rosary, Spellman. The Legion of Decency, the Knights
of Columbus, the Curia, plastic statues, holy water, *Our
Sunday Visitor*" (Donald P. Costello).

We are admonished to whore after "Julian Huxley,
Toynbee, and Malraux" (Rev. Robert T. Francoeur). We
are even served up peals of nunnish joy as "we pile into
the family station wagon for a lecture by Hans Kung or
Martin Luther King" (Sister Helen James John). We
are told about the crime of Georgetown for having booted
Mr. Francis E. Kearns out of the place (by—Mr. Francis
E. Kearns). Georgetown comes in for it again when we
are supposed to be shocked because the administration
saw to it that Madame Nhu would not be insulted when
she spoke there some months before the murder of her
family (the man who wanted to organize the hooters?
You guessed it again—lame duck Francis E. Kearns).

We watch a nice wringing of hands over university ad-
ministrators' reluctance to *force*—watch that verb!—
"participation in efforts for medicare and disarmament"
as well as whip into line those less than enthusiastic for
"peace marches, sit-ins, civil-disobedience ventures, and
other forms of dissent and protest" (Justice George Law-
ler). We are caught up in incense offered to "a greater
faith in the Teilhardian vision" with its "increased 'com-
plexification' of effort" (Lawlor again). And then there
is the poor devil at Notre Dame who complains that he
has never met a bishop in all his life. As any fool could

have told him the remedy consists in requesting an audience through the proper channels: I would suggest the Chancery.

And finally we run up against the High Priest of Dissent, Mr. Michael Novak, with his perpetual dissatisfaction with everything Catholic and most especially with not being Pope. He wags his long thin puritanical finger first at Paul VI for not having said all Novak (voice of the conscience of the Church) would have had him say about Catholic responsibility for historical guilt. Later we see the finger at work, wagging Novak style, at the last four hundred years of Catholic history which he considers to have been a mistake. He then keeps on wagging that long bone at the Italian Catholics, "childlike, irresponsible." He even wags with greater vehemence at the traditional Catholic doctrine concerning natural law: Novak won't buy natural law, although Aristotle, Plato, Cicero, Aquinas, Suarez and a number of pre-Novakian Catholics, as well as contemporary non-Catholics like Leo Strauss, have done so.

The trouble with *The Third Eye* is not that these boys (and girls) are nervous in the service, as we used to say back in World War II, but their nervousness is so crushingly monotonous. These writers—with the exception of Ned O'Gorman in his hauntingly beautiful "An Education for a Poet" and Garry Wills in his dissent to dissent —do not sing their Church. There is no pride in them. There is no thundering affirmation of the Church Triumphant. There is no adventure. These boys are not storming trenches. They are grousing behind the lines about the troops that surrounded them and that feed most of them.

I consider it ominous, not only for American Catholicism, but for American Christianity as such, that not a one of the whole gang says a word about the monstrous scandal of a third of the members of their own Church lying in Chains, lifting Christ again to the Cross in East Europe, a Cross formed by the lacerated flesh of millions who suffer slavery for His sake under the Sign of the Sin of our century. Not a one recalls Hungary and 1956, when in a lonely and splendid moment in American university history, thousands of young men offered themselves as volunteers in the most truly pure cause that

America could have embraced in this century. I shall
never forget how the whole student body of the University
of Santa Clara, to a man, signed a pledge forwarded to
President Eisenhower offering to go to their graves in
defense of that ravaged nation of heroes. I had never
been so proud of my brothers in the American Catholic
Church in all my life, but this kind of consideration is
alien to the writers with The Third Eye. Maybe they are
too young to remember 1956, but I have another theory
on the subject: I believe they are victims of a collective
act of forgetfulness because it is very difficult indeed to
look this century in the face without wavering. As a
result they have sought out a number of "objective cor-
relatives" in lesser causes upon which they could lavish
their Christian enthusiasm.

Not a one refers to the encirclement of the United
States by the enemy in his penetration into Southeast
Asia, Africa, and our own soft underbelly in South
America. The word Cuba is simply not to be found in
the whole book. These writers refuse to live within the
danger which forms the meaning of our moment in time.
The Third Eye look to other things: to books and to little
magazines; to sit-ins; and to dressing down or dressing
up the liturgy as though they were amateur sacristans,
past-Tractarians living in the security of Victorian England; to Martin Luther King and to Hans Kung. They
are busy, these latter-day Puritans who have dared to
take upon themselves the conscience of the Church. They
busy themselves—prigs that they are—in causes good,
indifferent, and bad that are altogether irrelevant to the
main business history has put on the agenda of the twentieth century.

But rather than launch into *that*, I would prefer to end
by writing down here the reaction of a Portuguese friend
of mine. He is part Negro but in my circles we do not
think about race; we think about Christ's Church in
agony. He has just now returned from the Congo where
he participated in the rescue of some dozens of white
men from savagery, but he went there to the jungles because he wanted to save the lives of missionary nuns.
This friend of mine is a *real* Catholic: when he read that
four Spanish sisters had been beheaded by the barbarians
and that dozens were hostages, he caught a plane to Africa

and got himself a gun—a submachine gun. Upon reading this book, he suggested that we burn it over champagne and cigars. We have set a date for this but before that I intend to go out and buy a plastic statue. I might add that when I get back to America I am going to sign up with the Knights of Columbus.

IV
**BIRTH
CONTROL**

The Birth Rate

WM. F. BUCKLEY JR.

The problem of birth control edges forward into the
political consciousness of America, as we come to recognize that it is not exclusively a moral issue. Although
it remains a private matter how many children a couple
chooses to procreate, it is increasingly apparent that the
decision that couple arrives at has considerable social
consequences. This is so merely in the commonplace
sense that families who beget more children than they
can afford to raise and educate end up impinging on the
precarious reserves that the affluent quite properly provide
for the indigent: in some countries that looms as the larg-
est consideration, but in others it does not. In such
countries as Nigeria it is a devastating fact that the birth
rate absorbs and then overcomes the increase in annual
productivity. In such countries the birth rate may be
decisive to economic health. In others—America for instance—it would be a long long time before the birth rate
so encumbered the rise in the gross national product as to
reverse its direction.

As regards the problem of the overpopulated countries,

new attention is being given to the moral and political problems. God, in His infinite wisdom, gave us, to be sure, the means by which to multiply the fishes and the loaves to a quite miraculous extent. A few dozen Iowa farmers could have fed all the Chosen Land, and the entire Roman Empire could have eaten well off the annual produce of the State of Minnesota. But the dour Dr. Malthus obstinately remarked that the earth is finite. We paid him no heed. In the exuberance of our productive glut we tended to assume that the procreative energies of the world could not possibly overtake our productive ingenuity. Well they have. And the world is up against it. In different ways, as I have remarked. Solutions for today and tomorrow are perhaps not so difficult to contrive—send tractors to India, and hybrid corn to Egypt. But the day after tomorrow?

There is a general stirring. There is, for instance, pressure against religious restrictions, or what are commonly thought of as such, against the dissemination of birth control information. In Connecticut, for instance, suit has been taken to the Supreme Court challenging the constitutionality of an old law against the use of contraceptives.[1] The issue is tangled up in religious prejudices: I say prejudices because a) it is commonly supposed, and indeed it is partly true, that the Catholic population of Connecticut stands adamant against the repeal of such a law, even though b) the law itself was passed a century ago at the urging of Protestant councils, and c) some very well known Catholic spokesman, for instance Fr. John Courtney Murray, oppose the law and wish for its repeal. In New York, a 75-year-old statute denying to the public welfare agencies the right to disseminate knowledge about the techniques of birth control is being circumnavigated by sophistical reasoning. And

---

1. The Court subsequently declared the law unconstitutional.

of course at the federal level we remember the anxiety of the Eisenhower Administration when faced with the question whether Point Four should include information about birth control.

The Catholic Church is, by common understanding, the bastion of resistance, because of its widely recognized stand against "birth control." In fact the Catholic Church is busily re-examining the premises of existing regulations on the subject. Meticulous moral theologians have carefully pointed out that the Church would not need to modify any existing dogma in order to sanction certain kinds of activity whose result would be birth control. What exactly that activity is, what are its limits, what are the moral consequences of the refinement of its position?—these are questions that thunder across the consciences of the most active theologians of the Church. Recently an English priest, going further than the accepted theology at the moment permits, was called to Rome for discipline, having blurted out his approval of contraceptive birth control. A Catholic doctor in Boston has written a book backing the use of regulatory pills as, in effect, agents of birth control, and although he has been perfunctorily disavowed by the hierarchy, he has not been exactly anathematized—precisely because the problem is undergoing a most intensive examination.

The fact of the matter is that a solution must be found. That old dog Malthus turned out to be very substantially correct in his dire predictions, and there seems to be no point in waiting until the United States is like India before moving in on the problem. It is axiomatic to the Christian faith that God did not burden us with any insoluble dilemmas, and that therefore He will grace the moral theologians with the insight into the correct solution. But the time-table is not necessarily of God's making: and all Christians must therefore think hard about the problem. Confident, yes, that a solution will suggest itself, but only insofar as they press forward in search for it— which they should do well before the day when, to press forward towards the solution of any problem, is to commit mayhem upon one's nearest neighbor.

Catholics and Population

GARRY WILLS

This is a hot one; fated to grow hotter. In fact, the closer men come to some control of the birth rate, the more intense will the conflicts with (and within) Catholicism become. Non-Catholics will predictably resent the action of men they must consider the last of the old-time detonators of our "population explosion." Some Catholics will just as predictably resent the intrusion of others in what they take to be a matter of personal conscience; they will anticipate a 1984 in which men can be punished for the Orwellian crime of "Overbirth." Other Catholics will resent the Catholics just described (and their hostility may be the bitterest of all).

The range and depth of Catholic reaction to this problem can be almost frightening. On the highest level of opposition, a theologian at one of America's most progressive seminaries says he must in conscience give up teaching if the official stand of Rome is altered—so little can he reconcile such alteration with the norms he has been taught, and has been teaching, throughout his scholarly career. At quite another level, an apocalyptic nincompoop in Ohio fires off letter after letter to all Catholic writers denouncing the enemies of God who want to rob Him of the babies He demands (as you see, the man's deity seems to resemble Moloch). In the name of orthodoxy, this ebullient boob concocts ingenious heresies—as when he writes that God needs men as "co-creators" and we are frustrating Him by not pulling the oar on our side. (There the weird crew-master sits, megaphoning at you and me and God, "Stroke! Stroke!")

Is anyone a fool, then, to rush into an area so clearly marked "Off Limits" for angels? It is no wonder that pacific men throw up their hands in despair and adopt this attitude. They feel that any attempt to clarify the matter will only confuse it. They have a point; most attempts have perhaps done this—not because of incompetence on the part of those Catholics who have suggested lines of development in the Church's teaching, but because it is so difficult to engage the real issues and so easy to ignite fiery resentment. In such a situation, a few minor flareups prompt my epistolary Savonarola to write that *devils* are rushing in where angels fear to tread; and the American bishops cancel a television series that simply presented the alternative views of Catholic theologians without advocating any single stand.

As I say, the difficulty is to engage the issue at all, to make minds mesh. In the coming debate, I am afraid that Americans generally must resign themselves to the task of acquiring some knowledge of the structure of Catholic thought. It is true that Catholic authority pronounces with full stringency only on revealed matters or on "natural truths" necessarily related to the revelation. But subsidiary guidance on moral problems is also given by the hierarchy; and this guidance has a binding quality extensively calibrated, ranging from very serious to very light. Such calibrations are easily blurred; the binding force of any teaching by authority is easily exaggerated. This is something the general public has had a taste of with regard to social encyclicals, where cries of "disloyalty" are used by Catholics on other Catholics. The same thing can be expected in the area we are dealing with.

Furthermore, aside from the hierarchic *social* structure of the Catholic teaching enterprise, the *content* of Christian teaching makes for a necessary resistance to change. The Catholic tradition is first of all an act of preservation of the revealed history of salvation; and, arising out of that first duty, it is an act of gradual *penetration* of further meanings contained in the redemptive history left to us in Scripture. The tradition advances, therefore, as a continued meditation on a set of events symbolic in themselves, and recorded in the further symbols of biblical style, and transmitted through the witness of many different ages (each using its own symbolic equipment of transmission). This means that Catholic thought involves an endless retracing of different strands in the traditional teaching. These strands unite and intertwine, and their entire force cannot be felt if isolated issues are dealt with. The economy of revelation must be considered as a whole; separate moral insights attain validity only as enunciated within this economy, as emerging out of a large and providential pattern, as interdependent with many other moral truths.

Obviously, this kind of consideration, spanning the centuries and using many different languages, is moral and ascetic and mystical as well as "philosophical" in the narrow sense. When a Christian school—the Augustinian, for instance, or the Thomist—moves some of the teaching out of its theological sphere and into a philosophic isolation, certain kinds of precision are achieved; but the entire effort must be resubmitted to the tradition, which has been formulated in the vocabulary of different ages and different schools without becoming identified with any one of them. Christian thinking develops, as Newman argued, not syllogistically but historically, by a reliving of the redemptive history in new eras.

At this point, impatient reader, you have a perfect right to your impatience. What has all this to do with the countdown on living-space? The clock is ticking, humanity is silting up on every continent, while I indulge in a theological revery. Yet it is just my point that these considerations are acutely relevant to the problem of engaging Catholics in a discussion of birth control. It is the most practical thing in the world to understand the sources of Catholic resistance to the general position of modern Americans and Europeans on contraception. Anything that has been part of the Catholic teaching or experience will not lightly be extruded from its place in that tenacious texture. And, whatever its technical status, the ban on contraceptives is clearly a large part of the Christian experience in modern times—(until *very* recent times, of Protestant as well as Catholic experience). Any religious norm that has worked itself into such a position has been related to the spiritual life in a thousand ways. This is especially true of a teaching with the obvious ascetic and social and familial repercussions of the ban on

contraceptives. The large family had become a kind of
badge of the Catholic faith; in a sense, it had its martyrs.
An important indictment was issued by many of those
holding this position: the rooted family, the view of love
as creative and outgoing, is in grating conflict today with
a hedonism that depends upon divorce, upon the total
mobility (and separability) of individuals, upon the destruction of woman's unique role and dignity, upon the
devaluation of the child to the level of an anchor imped-
ing that essential state of *drift* that contemporary man
lives in and for.

Of course, many people have stood up for the family
and for social duty without being Catholic or accepting
the Catholic position on birth control; but many Catholics have accepted that teaching precisely as the point
from which to oppose the atomistic tendencies of our
time, and their moral resistance to the world has been a
courageous and corrective one. Whatever can be said
against large families, there are spiritual values that were
customarily demanded and expressed in them; and we
must not be foolishly confident that we will keep the
values while dismissing their old matrix. It would be
faddism to reject the entire Christian witness involved in
the position of many Churches on this subject, or to mock
those who have upheld it (often at great personal cost, or
by extraordinary sacrifice).

As I say, these considerations all have tremendous
weight in a moral-theological tradition; but they are
bound to seem irrelevant to the man who wants to win a
vote for the public dispersion of condoms or pills without
being subjected to a course in Catholic theology. To him,
it will seem that Catholics are evading the issue or talking
about five other things when he only wants to talk about
point x or y. Sometimes, of course, they *will* be evading
the issue; but at other times they will be engaging it at the
points that are most vital to them, however tenuously
connected they may seem to others.

What, specifically, will Catholics be thinking about as
the public debate over birth control advances? Let me
list some of the concerns, valid and invalid, moving from
the most serious to the most trivial:

1. The preservation of authority, of the purity of doc-

trine, is obviously the prime concern of Catholic teaching authority as such. As a Christian, as a priest, as a man, a Pope will have concerns more humane and pastoral. But as a teacher he must keep the large symbolic revelation to man from becoming amorphous at its few points of fixity. Theologians must give him the instruments for maintaining this permanence of tradition. They, too, have a discipline not co-terminous with their own spiritual concerns. For such men, any change in the position of ecclesiastical authority at its most sensitive points—the authority of the Pope, and the authority of bishops.

There is no *ex cathedra* (infallible) papal pronouncement on the subject of contraceptives, but there are some very strong papal directives, including Pius XI's encyclical *Casti Connubii* (1930), which condemns "any use whatsoever of matrimony exercised in such a way that the act is deliberately frustrated in its natural power to generate life." The statement is, in its form, as solemn as anything to be found in encyclicals; and, since encyclicals have recently become popular, and great emphasis has effectively been put on their importance, it would disturb many to depart from this strongest papal teaching short of *ex cathedra* pronouncement. Others remark that it *is* short of infallible (and that this distinction has to *mean* something); that many past bulls and decrees of equal weightiness proved in time to be non-essential parts of the tradition; that the scriptural argument adduced in the encyclical is based on a misunderstanding of the Onan story; and that Church authority itself moved away from the strict interpretation of the encyclical when Pius XII approved the practice of "rhythm," which is certainly a deliberate attempt to use matrimony in such a way as to frustrate the individual sex act of its generative consequences.

2. The other area of authority affected by changes in the birth-control position is the *magisterium* (teaching office) of bishops. This *magisterium* is usually divided into "extraordinary" (pronouncements of the episcopal college assembled in a Council) and "ordinary" (the consensus of bishops exercising their teaching role around the globe). There has been no extraordinary teaching on the subject of birth control; but clearly the normal posi-

tion of the majority of bishops has for some time been one of opposition to the use of contraceptives. The tricky point here is that, although the Pope's ordinary teaching is not infallible, the ordinary teaching of the bishops is considered to be that of the Church itself, and therefore certain. Since this is a time when the idea of "collegiality" is being emphasized by theologians in order to counter the "papalism" of Vatican I, a consideration of the birth-control problem carries us into the whole tortured question of collegial authority. Is the question settled by the infallible consensus of the bishops in union with their head (Pius XI in his encyclical, Pius XII in various addresses)?

Those who think the question is *not* settled point out that a teaching of the *magisterium* cannot be casual. It must be considered, framed solemnly, and addressed precisely to the issue of *the magisterial weight to be given* a certain doctrine. A Pope, for example, must intend and say that he is pronouncing solemnly in order to do so. Some partial equivalent of this must exist when bishops form an infallible teaching, even of the "ordinary" sort. Otherwise, the unquestioned assumptions of any age would all become infallible by the fact that a majority of bishops hold them. These men point out that the conditions for conscious formulation of a magisterial teaching did not exist in the period of episcopal condemnation of contraceptives. For one thing, collegiality as a concept *was* in eclipse; most bishops were not exercising their own authority in conjunction with the Pope's, reaching a consensus after independent consideration; but simply relaying the Pope's instructions according to the papalist concepts of Vatican I. Furthermore, the challenge to the common position had not been framed in such a way that the response of authority was a reflective one based on thorough discussion. Yet formal definition comes in almost all cases as an answer to debate that presents the whole range of problems—again, to distinguish the ordinary magisterium from simple, unchallenged, widespread assumptions. And debate of the subtlety required for this problem is only now getting under way. In short, even the "ordinary teaching" of the bishops is obviously something more conscious and solemn than "common opinion." Otherwise a thousand questions treated as open to dispute would have been settled long ago by the homilies of a majority of the college.

3. Another concern of Catholics is with the concept of creation as good in itself and bearing traces of the Creator's intentions. This doctrine is, at its vital sources, a scriptural one; but Thomist theologians have framed the concept in philosophic terms drawn largely from Cicero's reporting of the Stoic arguments for a "natural law" in the universe. Thus anyone trying to understand the Catholic position on birth control must advert to the fact that there is a ticklish debate in progress over the various meanings of the term "natural law."

Put in its simplest terms, the Catholic argument has been this. The sex act is functional: it has its place in an amazing concatenation of physical processes that cooperate to produce a child. It has a *natural* purpose; and entirely to frustrate that purpose would be to go counter to the will of nature's Creator.

In its broad terms, all Catholic thinkers accept this position, though they would give different theoretical underpinnings to it and debate the meaning of terms like *"entirely* to frustrate." Disagreement begins with the application of this abstract rule to real situations. For instance, though procreation is the general end of marriage, must it be the specific end of each sex act? Moralists for years, indeed for centuries, held that it must; but a clear line of development has established that it need not be. Once it was considered sinful to have sex relations during pregnancy or after menopause because the act was divorced from conception in such circumstances. The great leap in the development of thought along these lines was the approval of "rhythm," which deliberately plans times when the individual sex act can be separated from procreation—plans it indeed with great care, vast expenditure of time, and skilled use of mechanical paraphernalia (thermometers, sugar tapes, charts). The *expertise* required by this system has even led some to charge that only the educated Catholic can have recourse to this approved method of family control—thus introducing a class distinction into sexual ethics.

Since all Catholics now hold that, for good reasons, men can separate the sex act from its consequences

(though this was expressly forbidden in *Casti Connubii*)
by *temporal* interposition, the question arises whether,
for the same good reasons, they may accomplish the
same thing, and do it more intelligently and efficiently,
by *medico-glandular* interposition (*e.g.,* the pill) or
physical interposition (*e.g.,* condoms or diaphragms).
The answer to this has so far been that in such circumstances the *end* is not being frustrated (any more than in
a successful rhythm scheme), but the very *nature of the
act* is violated. Note that this argument from "the integrity of the act" is *not* the argument of Pius XI against
frustrating the end of marriage. By their use of the term
"integrity" moralists suggest that there is only one natural
way to accomplish the sex act; that any other way of
doing it is a perversion which, like all perversions, de-
grades man. Opponents of this position answer that no
other physiological process has this ritual untamperability;
that it is, in fact, *natural* to man to transcend physical
limits by the use of intelligence (otherwise the whole
practice of medicine is "unnatural," as Christian Scientists
claim) and to turn brute functions to a higher use (otherwise the wine and carefully prepared banquet of good
fellowship are "unnatural" and we should all subsist on a
tasteless nutritional minimum); that it is characteristic
of the human sex act not to be limited only to fertile
periods and the necessities of survival but to have a
spiritual function as symbolic of married union (so that
"rhythm," by making intercourse a cyclic temporal phe-
nomenon, returns human sexuality to the bestial level);
that this symbolic function is a sufficient end for the sex
act during infertile periods or pregnancy or after menopause; that there is no reason why it should not be a
sufficient end when pills or contraceptives are used for the
same motives that justify the practice of rhythm; that the
only remaining objection to the use of these devices, as
opposed to the scientific exploitation of infertile periods,
is, in the case of the pill, a tabu about fiddling with reproductive system (a tabu constantly violated in common
medical practice) and, in the case of contraceptives, a
tabu about the untamperability of the intercourse process.
   This latter tabu has put some priests in the embarrassing position of creating a symbolic *spiritual necessity* for
the entrance of semen into the female reproductive sys-

tem in every act of intercourse—a necessity entirely separate (because of rhythm theory) from the immediate aim of procreation. One Jesuit put it this way in a recent book on the subject: "The woman who uses a diaphragm seals off physically the most intimate part of her body and thus, in symbol, closes the depths of her spirit to her husband." This physical cult of the female pudenda belongs in the textbooks of comparative anthropology. It is magic, and the priest-witchdoctor seems on the verge of prohibiting surgery because it would allow a doctor to penetrate "the depths of a woman's spirit." In fact, by this priest's "symbolic" standard of morality many women practicing rhythm are really married to their sugar-testers.

4. The conventional teaching is that procreation is the chief aim of intercourse, and pleasure a secondary one. Some fear that the separating of the sex act from the immediate possibility (or, as the irreverent might say, the immediate threat) of procreation will remove the pleasure from its subsidiary position. The answer to this is that the "primary-secondary" terminology looks, in a simplistic way conditioned by the cultural milieu of the Church Fathers, at the secondary aim as *sheer* physical pleasure, as an "indulgence," a "concession to concupiscence"; that the sex act, if it is used morally at all, is a human act expressive of love, of the shared joy with which man and woman become "one flesh"; that the marriage act is the natural superlative in the language of love and not simply a biological bribe to make men procreate; that, in this light, the "pleasure" and the procreation are aspects of a single thing. The proponents of the primary-secondary terminology think of the two aims as rivals, and maintain that the secondary aim must be reduced or "kept down" or minimized in all possible ways lest it cancel the "primary." One member of the Pope's study commission on birth control put it this way in a recent public interview. "I can't quite see opening up the act to greater love between the husband and wife and making this perhaps the more important end of marriage." Of course this attitude often masks a feeling that sexual pleasure is not the expression of human love but a rather inhuman concession to man's evil body. This view was

deeply imbedded in the works of the early Fathers, especially of the Platonist St. Augustine, and celibate theologians of the middle ages did not have the experience or the will to purge the tradition of these marks of cultural inadequacy. They have not been purged even yet. The current controversy shows, in embarrassing ways, that many Catholics defend the "natural law position" from motives that deny the very basis of the natural law—a belief that nature is good. (*America* magazine ran an article by a man who scorned intercourse as "the easy way" of showing love—and did this precisely in the name of what is "natural." He might as logically have scorned walking as the easy way to exercise the privilege of locomotion and advanced a "natural law" argument for walking on one's hands. This man would never have advocated the forswearing of conversation as an "easy way" of communicating with ones' spouse; his argument makes no sense except on the basis of a tacit belief that intercourse is not only "the easy way" but an ignoble way.)

5. Others oppose any discussion of "change," since the suggestion that the Church's teaching on this point is not perfectly formed will lead some Catholics, when they notice that theologians of standing believe the pill or other devices are moral, to follow their own consciences in this matter. The same response is to ask whether this is bad. Only those with a frivolous view of "Protestant" belief in the primacy of conscience think that Catholics have made, and will make, and should make decisions in the light of their own conscience as that is informed by all sources, revealed and authoritative and natural. No one has the right to prevent this; what one can do is make the conscience better informed—by all the means open to the reason of man. This, too, is part of the natural law.

6. The close texture of Catholic thought tends, at its best, to make people think in large terms, of the total balance, of the repercussion of any single view upon the spiritual lives of others. It also tends, at its worst, to a partisanship that does not treat issues according to their internal merits. People are for or against things because an Ottaviani or a Kung have taken this side or that. The

close fellowship of the Church turns into partisanship, making men decide theological matters on grounds that are primarily political, opposing or approving suggestions on birth control because they are "conservative" or "liberal." This trend should be noticed; but there is no need to dignify it with criticism.

7. Some argue that the social and spiritual consequences of encouraging the small family are undesirable, that this would be an encouragement of "selfishness." In some circumstances this might be true, but these are hardly grounds on which to decide a question of objective morality. Furthermore, the arguments for the large family are historically conditioned. Modern life puts severe demands upon parents and children which sheer *numbers* cannot solve (as they did in the days of hunting and physical struggle with a reluctant environment). In fact numbers add to the problems. Education is no longer a matter of putting a bow and arrow in a child's hand. The aim of marriage is children; not babies (as many as possible), but *children*—nurtured at the breast as well as in the womb, trained in and outside of schools, brought into an arena of severe spiritual challenge at each of those crises that make up the slow, complex maturation of the human animal in our time. The large family—often aided with tutors and nannies—was geared to survival at a different level. The duty toward children is often, today, a duty not to bring more children into a family in which the mother is overburdened already and able to give less than the proper amount of time to each of her offspring. Those Catholic women who are asking for a reconsideration of family life today are not ones who have no children and want none; they are precisely the mothers of children who would be cheated of even minimal attention by the immediate addition of more. In such circumstances, the true aim of marriage is itself the standard that requires parents to limit their families. This *is* marriage-as procreation. We are not put here to run quantitative fertility races.

8. Some argue that to alter one's theological perspective under the pressure of "overpopulation" is to make spiritual values give way to mere physical inconveniences.

They say that the demographic problems can be solved by technological means; that the truths of theology should not fluctuate under such vicissitudes; that any inconvenience caused during the lag between physical challenge and technological response must be borne as a testimony to man's superiority over his environment.

But this is not a simple question of finding food. This is a spiritual problem. Man, because he is man, develops skills and needs and demands, spheres of activity and awareness, that are increasingly subtle and complex; and "self-preservation" applies to these spiritual activities just as much as to physical limbs. The generation of life does not stop at the moment of conception or parturition or weaning; it extends to the development of the child's capacity for enjoying a truly human life in the context of humanity's current tasks and aspirations. This is true entirely apart from the physical crowding of the globe or the discovery of new foods.

9. Some argue that a change in the Catholic position on birth control would be a sign of, or would induce, an expanding permissiveness. The exaltation of the value of sex will, they say, lead to premarital intercourse, "petting," masturbation. The devices analysed and permitted will make extra-marital sex "too safe." This objection is the least justifiable of those we have considered, and one of the most common. In its essentials, it argues that truth should be suppressed for tactical reasons; that, whatever the force of arguments for or against contraceptives, men should be maintained in a safe ignorance. Adults should close their minds to anything that might cause trouble for tomorrow's adolescents. Admittedly, thinking is a dangerous occupation. But those who use arguments like these are not only trying to spare others the risks involved; they have forsworn the hazardous enterprise themselves.

The nine headings under which I have arranged a sampling of Catholic concerns are of course somewhat arbitrary. They could easily be doubled, rearranged, reduced to more basic matters. But these seem to me the most frequently proposed matters of debate, put in the terms that most often recur. Different Catholics, in different circumstances, will oppose new ideas on the end of

marriage as a threat to the Pope's authority, or to that of
bishops; as an offense against the natural law; as hedon-
istic, permissive, even "left-wing"; as substitution of selfishness for the spirit of sacrifice, or a premature concession to social difficulties. I think it must be clear by
now where my sympathies are in all these questions. But
I also want to make it clear that these are serious questions, with serious arguments on either side, and deep
spiritual consequences resting on the decision. The
decision should not be rushed; and those outside the
Church should muster whatever sympathies they can
while advancing the political and social claims the modern world can and must make upon the family.

For this is not a theological problem only. It is a
civil-social one—a fact that cuts two ways. We have
given the state great responsibility for the social welfare
of those brought into the world but unable to support
themselves. Under increasing pressure, the state is bound
to counter this with demands for responsibility to *it*. The
temptation to use means like sterilization to punish the
"indiscriminately fertile" will become severe. In such
circumstances, the boasted Liberal tolerance of individual
conscience will have to prove itself under fire. Catholics
and others who refuse to use contraceptives, to submit to
sterilization, to accept a eugenics code (or quota) dictated by the state, *must* have their freedom guaranteed,
even if this slows down the dreams of social planners.

On the other hand, Catholics must not try to inflict
their code on others (as they have in the past). The right
of conscientious objection is not the same as license for
sabotage. The rights of minorities should be protected;
but so should the rights of majorities. The social processes formulated by the many should be neither imposed on
the few nor frustrated by the few. Furthermore, though
others are bound to respect the freedom of Catholics in
this area, they have a right to demand a full and candid
discussion of Catholic citizens' attitudes toward every
aspect of the controversy. The rights of minorities cannot be recognized unless the extent of their claim is made
clear. Catholics as citizens can act to maintain their
moral freedom in this area; and they must, as citizens,
make clear to their fellow Americans the limits they place
upon their exceptional stand *vis-à-vis* the rest of our

society. This means, I believe, that there must be fewer
secret commissions, fewer canceled TV shows, fewer
Catholic attacks upon those who would discuss this
question outside the Curia or the chancery.

An Answer

L. BRENT BOZELL

National Review's discovery of the population explosion confirms *a*) that God's arrangements for peopling the planet have indeed gone awry, and if disaster is to be averted we had better grab the wheel quick; *b*) the means we employ are to be evaluated according to their efficiency; but *c*) let's face it—except maybe for abortion, voluntary methods haven't made a dent; so . . . *and*) Old Mother Hen can at last be counted on to get out of the way—though she may flap her wings a bit (obstructionists really "*must* have their freedom guaranteed") when the State moves as it is "bound" to, to enforce the imperatives of Survival. Oh, my. As to most of this, I assume the staff freedom philosophers will soon return from their vacations, and will have something to say, hopefully at the level of prudence, about an approach to the cosmos that points ineluctably to supervision of human generation by a State doctrinally forbidden to meddle with the postal service.

My main concern, however, is with Old Mother Hen, and with Garry Wills' assurances that she will not find her stubborn ways as difficult to mend as some of us had thought. The key problem: How to legitimatize contraceptives without compromising the integrity of the Catholic Church's teaching authority.

As to the Popes' teaching, the problem becomes manageable, on Wills' showing, as follows. (1) While "papal directives" on the subject are "very strong," none of them

is "infallible"—"including Pius XI's encyclical *Casti
Connubii* (1930), which condemns 'any use whatsoever
of matrimony exercised in such a way that the act is
deliberately frustrated in its natural power to generate
life.' " (2) The Church "moved away" from this teaching
"when Pius XII approved the practice of 'rhythm' ":
[separating] the sex act from its consequences . . . by
temporal interposition [was] expressly forbidden in *Casti
Connubii*." Therefore (3) the Church under Paul VI
is presumably at liberty to move away still further—to
the approval, say, of the interposition of condoms or pills.

1) Wills would have served us non-experts better by
allowing that his representation of *Casti Connubii* as
"not infallible" is at best a beleaguered point of view—
that a number of eminent theologians (*e.g.,* Cappello,
Gennaro, Piscetta, Tel Haar, Vermeersch) have expressly
held otherwise; while most of the other luminaries (*e.g.,*
Cartechini, Creusen, Zalba) have endorsed the technical
variant, as stated by the American authorities Ford and
Kelly that "Pius XI was clearly and solemnly declaring
a truth already infallibly taught by the Universal Church."

2) The contention that Pius XII's approval of "rhythm"
deviated from *Casti Connubii* is palpably not true—
palpably, that is, on the strength of the very passage of
Casti Connubii that Wills quotes: the sex act obviously
has no "natural power to generate life" during the
woman's infertile periods. A moment later, moreover,
Casti Connubi expressly condones the practice that Wills
advises was "expressly forbidden": "Nor are those considered as acting against nature who in the married state
use their right in the proper manner, although on account
of natural reasons *either of time* or of certain defects,
new life cannot be brought forth." (But did Pius XI, like
Pius XII, explicitly sanction a *systematic* exploitation of
the menstrual cycle? No: accurate knowledge of the
cycle's performance was not available until later on in
the thirties, after *Casti Connubii,* when the studies of the
Japanese, Ogino, and the Austrian, Knaus, first gained
general currency and acceptance.)

3) We can stand, I think, a fuller look at *Casti Connubii*. Provoked, among other things, by the collapse of the Anglican Church's opposition to contraceptives at Lambeth the previous summer, Pius XI wrote:

> The Catholic Church, to whom God has entrusted the defense of the integrity and purity of morals, standing erect in the midst of the moral ruin that surrounds her, in order that she may preserve the chastity of the nuptial union from being defiled by this foul stain, raises her voice in token of Divine Ambassadorship, and through Our mouth proclaims anew: Any use whatsoever of matrimony exercised in such a way that the act is deliberately frustrated in its natural power to generate life is an offense against the law of God and of nature, and those who indulge in such are branded with the guilt of a grave sin.

Noting that Pius met all of "the ordinary tests used by theologians" to determine infallibility, even Prof. John Noonan, whose recent history of the Church's teaching on contraception and related matters makes every possible bow to the possibilities of change, must ask: "If the Pope did mean to use the full authority to speak *ex cathedra* on morals, which Vatican I recognized as his, what further language could he have used?"

And we may ask the same about the unanimous teaching of the bishops, which Wills dismisses as mere "common opinion." What was missing when the Belgian bishops, for instance, issued a solemn pastoral letter on the subject in 1909? the Germans in 1913? the French, Austrian, and Americans in 1919?

All of which forces a pragmatic observation. If the Church next Monday were to abandon her teaching on contraceptives as set forth in *Casti Connubii*, I doubt whether the Church on Tuesday could plausibly hold herself forth, either to the faithful or to the world, as an infallible authority on morals—or on anything else except ghostly matters like the Assumption that are not subject to human disputation.

What, however, of anovulents? I don't know, and the

Church hasn't said. This is another ballgame. I own strong opinions about Christians' tampering with the generative process for any but pathological reasons; but *Casti Connubii* proscribes only the "use of matrimony"— the exercise of the sex "act"—under certain conditions; and pill-taking isn't sex. If the objection is that for this and that purpose condoms and pills come down to the same thing, the answer is that for this and that other purpose, they don't. And if the differences, for some, do not seem to justify a doctrinal distinction, the further answer is that while Mother Church always hopes for understanding by her children, she will settle for assent.

... and a Defense

GARRY WILLS

Mr. Bozell makes three points in answer to my article on "Catholics and Population."

First, he argues that *Casti Connubii* may, after all, have defined infallibly. It seems somewhat disingenuous of him (like quoting "it seems there is no God" as the position of St. Thomas) to give us John Noonan's question—If Pius XI had meant to define "what further language could he have used?"—without mentioning the two answers Noonan supplies on the same page. Pius VI could 1) have anathematized the contrary belief, which is the customary historical way of marking an obligation to believe, and/or 2) have stated directly his intention to define—as Pius XII did when enunciating the dogma of the Assumption. There is no doubt about this latter teaching's status—and one can reasonably say, in the light of Vatican I's delimitation of the infallible power, that if subsequent enunciations leave any doubt about the Pope's intention to define, then one must presume that he did *not* do so (a point made by Newman and Bishop Fessler in their expositions of the Vatican I teaching). Further arguments could be added to Noonan's: 3) Although the language of *Casti Connubii* is indeed strong, it is strongest

in terms of moral exhortation—for the Church to stand
up against a stain of impurity, and noticeably lacking a
declaration of what must be believed as a duty of orthodoxy, which is what is expressly enjoined in definition-
anathematization (*e.g.,* Pius XII on the Assumption: "We
pronounce, declare and *define* to be *divinely revealed
dogma*"). And 4) Pius XII flatly said that his pre-
decessors had not used the defining power in encyclicals
(*Hum. Gen.* par. 20). Pius' testimony is more impotant
than that of certain theologians of an older generation
with extreme papalist leanings. Mr. Bozell cites the names
of such theologians from Noonan—but he distorts his
source when he makes, on no evidence, the assertion
that "most other luminaries" have endorsed a merely technical variant of their view.

Mr. Bozell's second point is that restriction of intercourse to infertile periods does not fall under Pius' ban
against "any use whatsoever of matrimony" that deliberately frustrates the act's generative capacity "by human
effort," since the act does not have any generative capacity during infertile periods. But the Church recognizes the
overriding intention in marriage as capable of frustrating
the end of the marriage act (*cf.* Pius XII's condemnation
of rhythm used for selfish purposes); indeed, as capable
of entirely invalidating a marriage (if one partner had
the intention of using rhythm to block all conception).
The fact that the means used to circumvent the act's effect
is "merely" temporal does not affect the duty of having
procreation as one's marriage-intention with regard to the
act.

"Merely temporal" circumstances radically alter the
morality of human acts—*e.g.,* in the intercourse of two
partners on the day before and the day after their marriage, the act is physically the same but morally very
different. Pius XII obviously thought that rhythm frustrated the generative capacity of the act. In his famous

address on rhythm, he first contrasted it with practices that do *not* frustrate fertility, and then described rhythm as a suspension of "the *positive* and obligatory *carrying out of the act*" so that one "avoid(s) habitually the fecundity of the union." The act's "positive fulfillment may be omitted" for good reasons, as Pius recognized in his allocution; but his entire language for describing rhythm shows that, when it is used, the procreative end of marriage has been frustrated from its "positive carrying out" into generative consequence.

Third, Mr. Bozell argues, against my contention that the college of bishops did not define infallibly in this matter, that pastoral leters were issued in various countries. But 1) the Belgian episcopate of 1909 was not the whole college—nor were the other national bodies at the time they wrote. Nor 2) was the conception of collegial teaching consciously adhered to during the papalist atmosphere of the last century—yet an infallible teacher must *intend* to define. And 3) these pastoral letters are even more clearly made obsolete than *Casti Connubii* by Pius XII's approval of rhythm. The German letter says it is "serious sin to will to prevent *the increase of the number of children.* . . It is serious sin, very serious sin, *with whatever means and in whatever way it. occurs.*" The French letter condemned any attempt to "teach or encourage the restriction of birth." The American letter said births could never be limited for "pretended economic or domestic advantage." Every one of these teachings is expressly refuted in Pius XII's allocution. There is indeed a harmony between the pastorals Mr. Bozell relies on for establishing the Church (sic) teaching and the encyclical *Casti Connubii*, which said the aim of marriage is to give the Christian people "daily increase." Most of the pastoral letters were written, like the encyclical itself, at the prompting of Arthur Vermeersch. But this harmony does not prove Mr. Bozell's point—that the pastor-

als are, like the encyclical, infallible. Rather, it suggests
that the encyclical is, like the pastorals, obsolete at certain points—as obsolete as the *Syllabus of Errors*.

V

THEOLOGY
FOR MODERNS

The Death of God

HAROLD O. J. BROWN

While the general lay Christian reading public has an idea that Bonhoeffer, Bultmann, and Tillich have been saying deep and profound things about the Christian faith, the obscurity and inaccessibility of their real meaning has minimized the effect of their writing. It has remained for a former Cambridge University don, sometime New Testament scholar, and present bishop of Woolwich, Dr. John A. T. Robinson, to make their implications clear to the general public. That the general public is hungry for some kind of clarification of Christian concepts has been clearly indicated by the phenomenal sale, for a theological work, of his 141-page paperback *Honest to God,* which was the best-selling non-fiction work in England in 1963. Although in America the promotional value of having a bishop of the established church "publicly demonstrate that he is not a Christian" (London *Times*) is lacking, the American edition is also selling well.

Curiously, but typically enough, the interest in *Honest to God* and its author is being promoted by the clergy rather than by laymen. The book has been made the "Bible study and discussion" text for faculty members this year at Northfield School for Girls in Massachusetts, an institution founded by the American evangelist D. L. Moody. It is informative to contrast the differences in the welcome accorded Dr. Billy Graham at Harvard in

February with that prepared for Dr. Robinson's visit in
May. Dr. Graham, who is nothing if not orthodox in the
traditional sense of the word (*i.e.,* believing literally in
the orthodox, ecumenical creeds—the Apostles', Nicene,
and Chalcedonian—of the Christian church), found a
distinctly positive, if somewhat wary welcome from the
Roman Catholics, who are compelled from the logic of
their position to greet any orthodox Christian as a brother
and friend in the relativistic, largely atheistic or agnostic
climate of Cambridge. The majority of the Protestant
ministry, with two notable exceptions, were either downright hostile to him, denouncing him from his own plat-
form in the course of their "introductions" and in the
student *Crimson,* or at best frigidly neutral. He received
no opportunity to speak in the Harvard Memorial Church,
and it was made abundantly clear that the United Ministry at Harvard and Radcliffe neither supported, endorsed, nor approved of him. Robinson's arrival in May,
however, was for the first "United Ministry Forum,"
with University Preacher Charles Price announcing "full
cooperation."

What is this *Honest to God,* to become a best-seller in
England and to receive the enthusiastic promotion of a
large number of American churchmen and theologians?
Simply stated, it is the popularization of the theology of
Tillich, Bultmann, and Bonhoeffer, chiefly that of Tillich.
Honest to God takes Christian doublethink out of the
seminaries and puts it into the parishes. (A few years
ago the present dean of an Eastern school of theology
remarked in class, "When I am in church, I talk about
God. When I am with you, I say 'ultimate concern.'")

First, following Bultmann and Tillich, he seeks to pin
on the Bible and historic Christianity the concept of a
three-storey universe: Heaven above, earth in the middle,
and Hell below. Certainly such a view is found in
mediaeval woodcuts, but hardly in the teachings either of
the first Christian thinkers, such as Justin Martyr, a converted pagan philosopher, Irenaeus of Lyons, or the great
Alexandrian Christian scholars Clement and Origen, or
of the mediaeval theologians like Anselm of Canterbury, Peter Lombard, Thomas Aquinas. In his chapter
on Jesus Christ he charges that historic orthodoxy implies
that "Jesus was not really one of us; but through the

miracle of the Virgin Birth he contrived to be born so as to appear one of us." This entirely overlooks the first four centuries of Christian thought culminating in the Creed of the Council of Chalcedon (451 A.D.) with its clarion assertion that Jesus Christ is perfect man, in all things like unto us.

After presenting this caricature of Biblical and Christian thought, and stating that it is obviously unacceptable to modern man, Robinson suggests in place of the God of the Bible Tillich's ground of being: "The name of this infinite and inexhaustible depth and ground of all being is *God*. That depth is what the word *God* means . . . He who knows about depth knows about God." His second chapter, "The End of Theism?", makes it clear that God can no longer be considered in any sense personal. While it may be true enough that Christians tend to limit their concept of God by drawing too close an analogy with themselves as persons, this danger is certainly less destructive than Tillich's and Robinson's alternative, which is to deprive God of personality. The God of the Bible is at the very least as personal as we are. Tillich repudiates this concept of God, although ambiguously. Robinson's repudiation is unambiguous.

With the loss of any concept that God is personal, three basic dimensions of historic Christian thought disappear: revelation, relationship, and responsibility. Revelation, as a personal communication from God to man of something of His nature, will, and love, disappears, because while a personal God might conceivably have something to say to His creatures, the impersonal "ground of all being" neither can nor does. Thus the Christian Scriptures, and in fact all definite Christian concepts of any kind whatsoever become meaningless, because an unperson cannot communicate. Similarly, the idea of a relationship to God becomes absurd. In Chapter 5, "Worldly Holiness," prayer becomes more or less talking to oneself, in honesty indeed, but nonetheless to oneself.

The next-to-last chapter, "The New Morality," makes it clear that responsibility has likewise evanesced with the concept of the personal God of historic Christianity. It is not surprising that the consequences appear in today's world; what is surprising is that they appear in a book by a bishop under the guise of Christian teaching. In Rob-

inson's sixth chapter, all morality becomes completely
relative, a conclusion already anticipated by Hitler and
the dialectical materialists. However, Hitler and the
materialist Communist felt it necessary to challenge the
Christian Church; perhaps if they had had patience, they
could have beheld it destroying itself. John A. T. Robinson's seductive words, "Man has come of age," bear a
curious resemblance to those of the serpent in the Garden
of Eden: "Ye shall be like gods. . . ."

Honest to God represents a serious Protestant attempt
to realize Nietzsche's assertion, "God is dead. You have
killed Him." Lest other Christians, notably Roman Catholics, too glibly rejoice that "I am not like other men,
even as this publican," let it be pointed out that the
theology of Tillich, Bultmann, *et al,* roundly thrown out-
of-doors by the Church of Rome when it came boldly
knocking two or three decades ago, is now turning up in
the oddest places . . . even at the Vatican Council. An
orthodox creed and orthodox liturgy are no defense
against the depersonalization of God, as Bishop Robinson of the Church of England demonstrates. On the local
level, ambiguity is evident in Catholic thought: while
the Harvard Catholic chaplains were cordial to Billy
Graham, they will also be cordial to Robinson. Charity
is commendable, but we also have St. John's admonition,
"If there come any unto you, and bring not this doctrine
[*i.e.,* that Jesus Christ is the incarnate divinity, which
John has just expounded] receive him not into your house,
neither bid him God speed: for he that biddeth him God
speed is partaker of his evil deeds." (II John 10-11).

The ailment does not seem to be confined to Protestants
(would that it were!), but one common to modern Western post- or sub-Christian civilization. There is no question but that the historic Christian faith does not have the
hold on people that one might wish, nor does it appeal as
readily as one might hope. But the solution is not to
follow Robinson in demolishing the faith, so that there
will be nothing to which twentieth-century man can object, but to recognize, with Professor Walter Thorson of
MIT, that "if historic Christianity is in conflict with the
twentieth century, something is wrong with the twentieth
century."

The New Morality

SIR ARNOLD LUNN

The power-house of what has come to be known as the New Morality is believed by many to be the diocese of Southwark, of which Dr. Mervyn Stockwood is the dynamic Bishop. What the *Observer* of April 1, 1962 flippantly described as "Mervyn's Caravan" includes Dr. John Robinson, the Bishop of Woolwich, whose provocative *Honest to God* has sold over 100,000 copies, Canon Douglas Rhymes, and Canon Stanley Evans.

The Bishop of Southwark has given an impressive account of the problems which confronted him when he took over his immense diocese. "I decided that new methods would have to be used to break down the barriers of misunderstanding and apathy. Somehow the Church had to convince the man in the street that Christianity was relevant. It was a tough assignment. I had parishes of over 10,000 with congregations of less than 100, in many cases less than fifty." In face of this difficulty he decided to gather young men of initiative and independent ideas and give them their heads. "I encourage people with ideas, not necessarily ideas compatible with my own or with orthodox clerics," he remarked to a *Sunday Times* reporter. "My diocese is said to be 'on the boil.' If that is so I accept it as compliment. Boiling water is better than tepid; it can generate power and make it clean."

The Bishop and I have been friends for years. When he was the University Chaplain he invited me, a Roman

Catholic, to speak in the University Church, clear evidence that he is not unduly overawed by convention. A few days before this article was written he dined at my home and I do not think I am being indiscreet if I state that it would be very foolish to assume that the Bishop agrees with the more eccentric views expressed by members of "Mervyn's Caravan." He is, in fact, orthodox about the main articles of the Christian creed.

There is an excellent chapter on the most famous member of "Mervyn's Caravan," the Bishop of Woolwich, in an outstanding book, *The Secularization of Christianity,* by an Anglican theologian, Professor E. L. Mascall. Professor Mascall does not agree with the author of an article in *Encounter* who boldly states that "what is striking about Dr. Robinson's book is that he is an atheist." On the contrary he admits to a suspicion, which I share, that Dr. Robinson is "after all really an old-fashioned Christian theist" and he explains his eccentricities by suggesting that Dr. Robinson "had despaired of trying to convert the world to Christianity and had decided instead to convert Christianity to the world." The Archbishop of Canterbury left the convocation of Canterbury in no doubt about his views of *Honest to God.* On May 8, 1963 he said:

> We are asked to think that the enterprise was a matter of being 'tentative,' 'thinking aloud,' 'raising questions,' and the like. But the initial method chosen was a newspaper article, crystal clear in its argument, and provocative in its shape and statement, to tell the public that the concept of a personal God as held both in popular Christianity and in orthodox doctrine is outmoded, and that atheists and agnostics are right to reject it.

But it is not with the Bishop of Woolwich's confused theology that we are chiefly concerned but with his view on morality. He rejects the theory that there are absolute standards ordained by God "engraven for all to see." "It is," comments the Archbishop of Canterbury, "on a deductive theory from the concept of love and not upon a full examination of Christ's teaching that the conclu-

sion is being drawn that 'nothing of itself can be labelled wrong.'" "One cannot, for instance," writes the Bishop of Woolwich, "start from the position that sex relations before marriage or divorce are wrong or sinful in themselves. They may be in 99 cases out of a 100 or even 100 out of 100, but they are not intrinsically so, for the only intrinsic evil is lack of love." Mr. R. J. B. Eddison in the course of a very friendly review in the *Church of England Newspaper* (March 6, 1964) of *The New Morality*, a book I wrote in collaboration with an Anglican, Garth Lean, speaks to this point: "What this book seems to me to do so effectively is to nail the heresy that love has in some way nullified the law. This is not what the New Testament teaches us. 'Love,' it says, 'is the fulfilling of the law.' In other words, because we love, we shall observe the precepts of the law all the more carefully. We might as well argue that care on the roads is a substitute for the highway code."

The real inspiration of the New Morality is the uneasy belief that the time has come to substitute democracy for theocracy in sexual morality.. "It is very little use," writes Canon Douglas Rhymes, "to have a morality that will only be taken notice of by two per cent of nation. The moral law today is being ignored because it is already out-dated" (*Church Times*, March 22, 1963). The contrast between traditional Christianity and this new Christianity, which changes as public opinion changes, corresponds roughly to the difference between absolute and constitutional monarchy. For the traditional Christian God is an Absolute Monarch whose laws do not require human endorsement and must continue to command our unqualified obedience even if only Canon Rhymes' two per cent of the nation are Christian. For the constitutional theist God can only act on the advice of his clerical Ministers who will see to it that his moral laws change with the changing views of the human electorate.

Is there, however, any reason to suppose that the Churches will make more converts if they relax their standards? Is it not far more likely that the young will merely suspect that those who are so ready to compromise on the fundamentals of Christian belief have lost confidence in their ability to defend the faith? The basis of their argument is the false assumption that the modern world in general and modern youth in particular have no use for the traditional Christian morality. Young men have always found it difficult to be chaste, but there is a world of difference between failing invariably to live up to the exacting Christian code and attacking the code itself; and it was against the intellectual immorality of the middle-aged rather than the physical immorality of some of the young that Garth Lean and I directed our attack. There will always be a big lag between the standards a society officially approves and the standard of average behaviour; but if the official standards are lowered, the practice is correspondingly lowered.

It is because this is instinctively realised that a majority still resent any tampering with official standards. The *Sunday Telegraph* of August 4, 1963, revealed that a "Gallup Poll enquiry shows that less than one in four of the British public favour easier divorce." Three weeks later the same paper announced the result of a Gallup Poll concerning the statement by Dr. Peter Henderson, the Principal Medical Officer of the Ministry of Education, who said that young couples planning marriage are not unchaste if they have sex relations before marriage. Only 17 out of every hundred agreed; 66 disagreed and the remaining 17 replied "I don't know." "It would, of course, be optimistic," wrote the Editorial, "to conclude that all those who favour chastity practice it," but " 'enlightened' clergymen should not leap as easily as they sometimes do to the conclusion that the only thing that keeps people out of church is disapproval of Christian standards of sexual behaviour."

The results of various university debates confirm this view. Thus the Union Society Cambridge defeated by 263 votes to 209 on November 12, 1963 the motion "That 'till death do us part' is ridiculous," and on January 16, 1964 the Union Society, London University defeated by 282 votes to 189 the motion "That this house rejects the Christian conception of sex."

One interesting result of this New Morality campaign has been to produce a new alignment among Christians. My co-author in two books attacking this movement, *The New Morality* and *The Cult of Softness,* is an Anglican, who rightly feels that whereas he and I agree on fundamentals he is utterly opposed to those members of his own Church whose reinterpretation of Christianity in effect amounts to repudiation. Family differences between Christians are regrettable but relatively unimportant compared to the decisive struggle between Christians and secularists.

VI

THE
COUNCIL

The Same Again, Please

EVELYN WAUGH

It is unlikely that the world's politicians are following the concluding sessions of the Vatican Council with the anxious scrutiny given to its opening stages in 1869. Then the balance of power in Europe was precariously dependent on the status of the papal states in Italy; France and Austria directly, Prussia indirectly, and the Piedmontese kingdom particularly, were involved in their future. Even Protestant England was intent. Gladstone had his own personal theological preoccupations and was in unofficial correspondence with Lord Acton, but Lord Clarendon, the Foreign Minister, and most of the cabinet studied the despatches of their agent, Odo Russell, (lately selected and edited with the title of *The Roman Question*) and pressed him for the fullest details. Manning was privately dispensed of his vow of secrecy in order that he might keep Russell informed. Queen Victoria ruled as many Catholics as Anglicans, a section of whom in Ireland were proving increasingly troublesome.

The Council, as is well known, adjourned in dramatic circumstances which seemed to presage disaster. Subsequent history confirmed its decisions. The Paris Com-

mune obliterated Gallicanism. Bismarck's *Kulturkampf*
alienated all respectable support of the dissident Teutons.
All that Odo Russell had consistently predicted came
about in spite of the wishes of the European statesmen.

The consultations resumed after their long recess and
dignified by the title of the Second Vatican Council are
not expected to have the same direct influence outside
the Church. The popular newspapers have caught at
phrases in the Pope's utterances to suggest that there is
a prospect of the reunion of Christendom. Most Christians, relying on the direct prophecies of Our Lord, expect
this to occur in some moment of historical time. Few
believe that moment to be imminent. The Catholic
aspiration is that the more manifest the true character of
the Church can be made, the more dissenters will be
drawn to make their submission. There is no possibility
of the Church's modifying her defined doctrines to
attract those to whom they are repugnant. The Orthodox
Churches of the East, with whom the doctrinal differences
are small and technical, are more hostile to Rome than
are the Protestants. To them the sack and occupation of
Constantinople for the first half of the thirteenth century
—an event which does not bulk large in the historical
conspectus of the West—is as lively and bitter a memory
as is Hitler's persecution to the Jews. Miracles are possible; it is presumptuous to expect them; only a miracle
can reconcile the East with Rome.

With the Reformed Churches, among whom the
Church of England holds a unique position in that most
of its members believe themselves to be a part of the
Catholic Church of the West, social relations are warmer
but intellectual differences are exacerbated. A century
ago Catholics were still regarded as potential traitors, as
ignorant, superstitious and dishonest, but there was common ground in the acceptance of the authority of Scripture and the moral law. Nowadays, I see it stated, representative Anglican clergymen withhold their assent to
such rudimentary Christian tenets as the Virgin birth and
resurrection of Our Lord; in the recent prosecution of

Lady Chatterley's Lover two eminent Anglican divines gave evidence for the defense, one of them, a bishop, in the most imprudent terms. Another Anglican dignitary has given his approval to the regime which is trying to extirpate Christianity in China. Others have given their opinion that a man who believes himself threatened by a painful death may commit suicide. Aberrations such as these, rather than differences in the interpretation of the Augustinian theory of Grace, are grave stumbling blocks to understanding.

It is possible that the Council will announce a defini-tion of the *communicatio in sacris* with members of other religious societies which is forbidden to Catholics. Rigour is the practice of some dioceses, laxity of others. There is no universal rule, for example, about the celebration of mixed marriages. On the other hand some French priests, in an excess of "togetherness," are said to administer Communion to non-Catholics, an imprudence, if not a sacrilege, which can only be reprobated. The personal cordiality shown by the Pope to Protestants may well be the prelude to official encouragement to cooperate in social and humanitarian activities, which would remove the bitterness from a condemnation of association in the sacraments.

The question of Anglican Orders is unlikely to be raised, but it is worth noting that the conditions have changed since their validity was originally condemned. Then the matter was judged on the historical evidence of the Reformation settlement. But since then there have been goings-on with *episcopi vagantes,* Jansenist Dutch and heterodox eastern bishops, with the result that an incalculable proportion of Anglican clergymen may in fact be priests. They may themselves produce individual apostolic, genealogical trees, but the results will be of little interest to the more numerous Protestant bodies to whom the Pope's paternal benevolence is equally directed.

A Catholic believes that whatever is enacted at the Council will ultimately affect the entire human race, but its immediate purposes are domestic—the setting in order

of the household rudely disturbed in 1870. There are
many questions of great importance to the constitution
of the Church which do not directly affect the ordinary
Catholic layman—the demarcation of dioceses, the
jurisdiction of bishops, the setting to contemporary uses
of the powers of the ancient religious orders, the changes
necessary in seminaries to render them more attractive
and more effective, the adaption of missionary countries
to their new national status, and so forth. These can
safely be left to the experience and statesmanship of the
Fathers of the Council. But in the preliminary welcome
which the project has enjoyed during the past three years
there has been an insistent note that the "Voice of the
Laity" shall be more clearly heard and that voice, so far
as it has been audible in northern Europe and the U.S.,
has always been largely that of the minority who demand
racial reform. It seems to me possible that many of the
assembled Fathers, whatever their own predilections, have
an uneasy feeling that there is a powerful body of the
laity urging them to decisions which are, in fact, far from
the hopes of the larger but less vocal body of the faithful.

I speak for no one but myself but I believe I am fairly
typical of English Catholics. The fact that I was brought
up in another society does not embarrass me. I have been
a Catholic for thirty-two of what are technically known
as my "years of reason"; longer, I think, than many of
the "progressives"; moreover I think that a large proportion of European Catholics, despite their baptisms and
first communions, are in fact, "converts" in the sense
that there came to them at some stage of adolescence or
maturity the moment of private decision between acceptance and rejection of the Church's claims.

I believe that I am typical of that middle rank of the
Church, far from the leaders, much further from the
saints; distinct too from the doubting, defiant, despairing
souls who perform so conspicuously in contemporary
fiction and drama. We take little part, except where our
personal sympathies are aroused, in the public life of the
Church, in her countless pious and benevolent institu-

tions. We hold the creeds, we attempt to observe the
moral laws, we go to Mass on days of obligation and
glance rather often at the vernacular translations of the
Latin, we contribute to the support of the clergy. We
seldom have any direct contact with the hierarchy. We
go to some inconvenience to educate our children in our
faith. We hope to die fortified by the last rites. In every
age we have formed the main body of "the faithful" and
we believe that it was for us, as much for the saints and
for the notorious sinners, that the Church was founded.
Is it our voice that the Conciliar Fathers are concerned
to hear?

There are three questions of their authority which
sometimes come to our attention.

One is the Index of Prohibited Books. I have been told
that its promulgation depends on the discretion of the
diocesan bishop. I do not know if it has been promul-
gated in my diocese. It is not at all easy to obtain a copy.
When found, it is very dull, consisting largely of pam-
phlets and these on forgotten controversies. It does not
include most of the anthropological, Marxist and psychological theses which, uncritically read, might endanger
faith and morals. Nor, as is popularly believed, does it
include absurdities like *Alice in Wonderland*. There are
a few works, such as Addison's essays, which one expects
to find in any reputable home and several which are
compulsory reading at the universities, but in general, it
is not a troublesome document. Sartre's presence on the
list provides a convenient excuse for not reading him.
But there is an obvious anomaly in preserving a legal
act which is generally disregarded. I think most laymen would be glad if the Fathers of the Council would
consider whether it has any relevance in the modern
world; whether it would not be better to give a general
warning of dangerous reading and to allow confessors to
decide in individual cases, while retaining particular
censorship only over technical books of theology which
might be mistaken for orthodox teaching.

A second point is the procedure of ecclesiastical courts.

Most laymen spend a lifetime without being involved with them, just as they live without acquaintance with criminal proceedings. Cases of nullity of marriage are, however, becoming more common and much vexation and often grave suffering is caused by the long delays which result from the congestion of the courts and their laborious methods. The layman does not question the authority of the law or the justice of the decision; it is simply that when he finds himself in doubt, he thinks that he should know in a reasonable time his precise legal status.

Thirdly, it would be satisfactory to know the limits of the personal authority held by the bishop over the laity. No vows of obedience have been made. Not in England, but in many parts of the world it is common to see a proclamation enjoining the faithful "on pain of mortal sin" to vote in a parliamentary election or abstain from certain entertainments. Have our bishops in fact the right to bandy threats of eternal damnation in this way?

As the months pass and the Council becomes engrossed in its essential work, it is likely that the secular press will give less attention to it than it has done to its spectacular assembly. The questions for discussion are a matter of speculation to all outside the inner circle but there is a persistent rumour that changes may be made in the liturgy.

I lately heard the sermon of an enthusiastic, newly ordained priest who spoke, perhaps with conscious allusion to Mr. Macmillan's unhappy phrase about Africa, of a "great wind" that was to blow through us, sweeping away the irrelevant accretions of centuries and revealing the Mass in its pristine, apostolic simplicity; and as I considered his congregation, closely packed parishioners of a small country town of whom I regard myself as a typical member, I thought how little his aspirations corresponded with ours.

Certainly none of us had ambitions to usurp his pulpit. There is talk in Northern Europe and the United States of lay theologians. Certainly a number of studious men

have read deeply in theology and are free with their
opinions, but I know of none whose judgment I would
prefer to that of the simplest parish priest. Sharp minds
may explore the subtlest verbal problems, but in the long
routine of the seminary and the life spent with the
Offices of the Church the truth is most likely to emerge.
It is worth observing that in the two periods when laymen took the most active part in theological controversy,
those of Pascal and Acton, the laymen were in the wrong.

Still less did we aspire to usurp his place at the altar.
"The Priesthood of the Laity" is a cant phrase of the
decade and abhorrent to those of us who have met it.
We claim no equality with our priests, whose personal
feelings and inferiorities (where they exist) serve only
to emphasize the mystery of their unique calling. Anything in costume or manner or social habit that tends to
disguise that mystery is something leading us away from
the sources of devotion. The failure of the French
"worker priests" is fresh in our memories. A man who
grudges a special and higher position to another is very
far from being a Christian.

As the service proceeded in its familiar way I won-
dered how many of us wanted to see any change. The
church is rather dark. The priest stood rather far away.
His voice was not clear and the language he spoke was
not that of everyday use. This was the Mass for whose
restoration the Elizabethan martyrs had gone to the
scaffold. St. Augustine, St. Thomas a Becket, St. Thomas
More, Challoner and Newman would have been perfectly
at their ease among us; were, in fact, present there with
us. Perhaps few of us consciously considered this, but
their presence and that of all the saints silently supported
us. Their presence would not have been more palpable
had we been making the responses aloud in the modern
fashion. It is not, I think, by a mere etymological con-
fusion, that the majority of English-speaking people believe that "venerable" means "old." There is a deep-lying
connexion in the human heart between worship and age.

But the new fashion is for something bright and loud

and practical. It has been set by a strange alliance between archeologists absorbed in their speculations on the
rites of the second century, and modernists who wish to
give the Church the character of our own deplorable
epoch. In combination they call themselves "liturgists."
The late Father Couturier, the French Dominican, was
very active in designing aids to devotion, but tourists are
more common than worshippers in the churches he inspired. At Venice there is a famous little chapel designed
in his extreme age by Matisse. It is always full of sight-
seers and the simple nursing sisters whom it serves are
proud of their acquisition. But the Stations of the Cross,
scrawled over a single wall, are so arranged that it is
scarcely possible to make the traditional devotions before
them. The sister in charge tries to keep the trippers from
chattering but there is no one to disturb; on the occasions
I have been there I have never seen anyone in prayer,
as one always finds in dingy churches decorated with
plaster and tinsel.

The new Catholic cathedral in Liverpool is circular in
plan; the congregation are to be disposed in tiers, as
though in a surgical operating theatre. If they raise their
eyes they will be staring at one another. Backs are often
distracting; faces will be more so. The intention is to
bring everyone as near as possible to the altar. I wonder
if the architect has studied the way in which people take
their places at a normal parochial Mass. In all the
churches with which I am familiar it is the front pews
which are filled last.

During the last few years we have experienced the
triumph of the "liturgists" in the new arrangement of the
services for the end of Holy Week and for Easter. For
centuries these had been enriched by devotions which
were dear to the laity—the anticipation of the morning
office of Tenebrae, the vigil at the Altar of Repose, the
Mass of the Presanctified. It was not how the Christians
of the second century observed the season. It was the
organic growth of the needs of the people. Not all
Catholics were able to avail themselves of the services

but hundreds did, going to live in or near the monastic houses and making an annual retreat which began with Tenebrae on Wednesday afternoon and ended at about midday on Saturday with the anticipated Easter Mass. During these three days time was conveniently apportioned between the rites of the Church and the discourses of the priest taking the retreat, with little temptation to distraction. Now nothing happens before Thursday evening. All Friday morning is empty. There is an hour or so in church on Friday afternoon. All Saturday is quite blank until late at night. The Easter Mass is sung at midnight to a weary congregation who are constrained to "renew their baptismal vows" in the vernacular and later repair to bed. The significance of Easter as a feast of dawn is quite lost, as is the unique character of Christmas as the Holy Night. I have noticed in the monastery I frequent a marked falling off in the number of retreatants since the innovations or, as the liturgists would prefer to call them, the restorations. It may well be that these services are nearer to the practice of primitive Christianity, but the Church rejoices in the development of dogma; why does it not also admit the development of liturgy?

There is a party among the hierarchy who wish to make superficial but startling changes in the Mass in order to make it more widely intelligible. The nature of the Mass is so profoundly mysterious that the most acute and holy men are continually discovering further nuances of significance. It is not a peculiarity of the Roman Church that much which happens at the altar is in varying degrees obscure to most of the worshippers. It is in fact the mark of all the historic, apostolic Churches. In some the liturgy is in a dead language such as Ge'ez or Syriac; in others in Byzantine Greek or Slavonic which differ greatly from the current speech of the people.

The question of the use of the vernacular has been debated until there is nothing new left to be said. In dioceses such as some in Asia and Africa where half a dozen or more tongues are spoken, translation is almost impossible. Even in England and the United States where much the same language is spoken by all, the difficulties are huge. There are colloquialisms which, though intelligible enough, are barbarous and absurd. The vernacular used may either be precise and prosaic, in which case it has the stilted manner of a civil servant's correspondence, or poetic and euphonious, in which case it will tend towards the archiac and less intelligible. The Authorized Version of the Bible of James I was not written in the current tongue but in that of a century earlier. Mgr. Knox, a master of language, attempted in his translation of the Vulgate to devise a "timeless English" but his achievement has not been universally welcomed. I think it highly doubtful whether the average church-goer either needs or desires to have complete intellectual, verbal comprehension of all that is said. He has come to worship, often dumbly and effectively. In most of the historic Churches the act of consecration takes place behind curtains or doors. The idea of crowding round the priest and watching all he does is quite alien there. It cannot be pure coincidence that so many independent bodies should all have evolved in just the same way. Awe is the natural predisposition to prayer. When young theologians talk, as they do, of Holy Communion as "a social meal" they find little response in the hearts or minds of their less sophisticated brothers.

No doubt there are certain clerical minds to whom the behaviour of the laity at Mass seems shockingly unregimented. We are assembled in obedience to the law of the Church. The priest performs his function in exact conformity to rules. But we—what are we up to? Some of us are following the missal, turning the pages adroitly to introits, and extra collects, silently speaking all that the liturgists would like us to utter aloud and in unison. Some are saying the rosary. Some are wrestling with refractory children. Some are rapt in prayer. Some are thinking all manner of irrelevant things until intermittently called to attention by the bell. There is no apparent "togetherness." Only in heaven are we recognizable as the united body we are. It is easy to see why some clergy would like us to show more consciousness of one another, more evidence of taking part in a social "group activity." Ideally they are right, but that is to pre-suppose a very much deeper spiritual life in private than most of us have achieved.

If, like monks and nuns, we arose from long hours of meditation and solitary prayer for an occasional excursion into social solidarity in the public recitation of the office, we should, unquestionably, be leading the full Christian life to which we are dedicated. But that is not the case. Most of us, I think, are rather perfunctory and curt in our morning and evening prayers. The time we spend in church—little enough—is what we set aside for renewing in our various ways our neglected contacts with God. It is not how it should be, but it is, I think, how it has always been for the majority of us and the Church in wisdom and charity has always taken care of the second-rate. If the Mass is changed in form so as to emphasize its social character many souls will find themselves put at a further distance from their true aim. The danger is that the Conciliar Fathers, because of their own deeper piety and because they have been led to think that there is a strong wish for change on the part of the laity, may advise changes that will prove frustrating to the less pious and the less vocal.

It may seem absurd to speak of "dangers" in the Council when all Catholics believe that whatever is decided in the Vatican will be the will of God. It is the sacramental character of the Church that supernatural ends are attained by human means. The inter-relation of the spiritual and material is the essence of the Incarnation. To compare small things with great, an artist's "inspiration" is not a process of passive acceptance of dictation. At work he makes false starts and is constrained to begin again, he feels impelled in one direction, happily follows it until he is conscious that he is diverging from his proper course, new discoveries come to him while he is toiling at some other problem, so that eventually by trial and error a work of art is consummated. So with the inspired decisions of the Church. They are not revealed by a sudden clear voice from Heaven. Human arguments are the means by which the truth eventually emerges. It is not really impertinent to insinuate one more human argument into the lofty deliberations.

Open Season
on the Church

WILL HERBERG

I have come to the reluctant conclusion that *aggiorna-mento* (updating, bringing up to date), the slogan under which the Second Vatican Council has received its major publicity, is both unsound and mischievous. It has not been an easy conclusion to come to. Like so many others, I have been inclined to feel nothing but enthusiasm and gratitude for the Council and its work. I still am; but the slogan *aggiornamento,* which is supposed to describe the very spirit of the Council, troubles me greatly.

There is little doubt in my mind that the Second Vatican Council, by its being as well as by its doings, will go down in history as one of the very great events of the century.

The Council has officially ended the "cold war" between Catholicism and Protestantism that was launched by Reformation and Counter-Reformation and raged for four-hundred years. It has given solid substance and magisterial approval to the movement of rapprochement, religious and social, among the divided forces of Christendom which had emerged out of the totalitarian crisis in Europe. It has adopted constitutions, decrees, and positions on a number of questions where a reassertion of Church teaching with a new clarity and emphasis seemed necessary. All this, and more, it seems to me, the whole world—or, at least, the whole well-disposed world—should welcome.

Yet I deplore the slogan under which so much of this was done; in fact, I regard this slogan as a standing threat to the achievements of the Council as achievements of the Church. *Aggiornamento,* I am convinced, has proved mischievous in its short-term effects, and must be adjudged false and unsound in longer-range terms as an attitude of the Church.

What do I find so wrong with the idea of *aggiornamento?* In the first place, it has been taken (and not without encouragement from high places) to mean that the Church, for the first time in centuries, is to be given a thorough housecleaning and made to discard its "outworn" and "old-fashioned" accumulation of possessions —"outworn" ideas, "outworn" institutions, "outworn" practices, even "outworn" beliefs. Naturally, everyone has had his own view of what is "outworn" and ought to be discarded; and so the slogan *aggiornamento* has become the signal for *open season on the Church.* Even the most cursory reading of the *aggiornamento* "Catholic" press in this country and abroad will reveal the scandalous lengths these *frondeurs* have permitted themselves to go. A book is published under the title *Honesty in the Church*; with all reservations and qualifications, what can this title mean but that only now, only in the blessed age of *aggiornamento,* can honesty raise its voice in the Church?

And the *National Catholic Reporter* (March 31, 1965) features a review of this book under a two-column heading, "HOPE THAT CENTURIES OF DOUBLE TALK END." The effrontery of this statement, in a "Catholic" journal by a "Catholic" editor, fairly takes one's breath away! For centuries—*centuries,* mark you—the Church has been handing out "double talk"; now, at last, in the blessed age of *aggiornamento* is there a "hope" that this kind of "double talk" will on the part of the Church end! I wouldn't treat a pawn shop or some advertising agency the way these "Catholics" find it possible to treat their Church.

The same journal (April 7, 1965) proudly features a full page of items under a decorative heading, "IDEAS TO ROCK THE BARQUE OF PETER." It is only in the blessed age of *aggiornamento* that rocking the boat of the Church can be recommended as a form of Catholic loyalty.

I will not permit myself to comment on *Ramparts,* another "Catholic" journal practicing *aggiornamento.* Anti-clerical snarling and leftist incitement constitute the bulk of the offerings of this sensation-mongering Liberal magazine. And all in the name of *aggiornamento!*

In short, under cover of *aggiornamento,* a *fronde* has been opened against the Church, which those vested with care for the welfare of the Church cannot afford to neglect.

But my objections to *aggiornamento* run deeper than just the exploitation of this slogan to declare an open season on the Church. The very idea behind this slogan seems to me to be radically wrong, and utterly unworthy of the Church.

Aggiornamento means updating, bringing up to date. However appropriate this might be for a commercial or industrial establishment, it hardly seems to be an obligation imposed upon the Church of Christ. It is part of the vocation of the Church of Christ (I should say) not to be forever adapting itself to the changing times, but to stand firm and resolute for the eternal truth about God, man, and the world over against the endlessly shifting panorama of intellectual fashion and social interest.

Over against? Yes, over against! It is for the Church, while receiving truth from whatever source it may come, to take a stand against the *Zeitgeist,* the spirit of the age —not just against this or that spirit of the age, but against every possible spirit of the age devised by man in history, because every possible spirit of the age devised by man in history, is an "imagination" devised by sinful man in a world waiting ("groaning," Paul says) for redemption.

The great Hilderbrand, (Gregory VII), nine hundred years ago, brushed aside the ideas of *aggiornamento*, and refused to allow the Church to update itself by adjustment to the feudal *Zeitgeist;* on the contrary, this greatest of all Popes fought a hard, often desperate, but in the end successful battle to disengage the Church from the feudal system, and thus to save the *Libertas Ecclesiae.* The Church has been less successful in keeping itself clear of nationalism, and perhaps also socialism—the two demonic political passions dominating our century, and combining to form totalitarianism.

That is why I am so uneasy about the vernacular liturgy, permitted, even recommended, by the Council. It has many advantages, of course; but, in the last analysis, what is it but another stage in the fragmentation of the universal substance of the Church along national-cultural lines? I am sorry to see the Latin go in this way, for Latin is not only the traditional texture of the Roman Catholic liturgy; Latin is truly a universal vehicle, since it is the living spoken language of no nation today. The slogan *aggiornamento* applied here and elsewhere suggests that there are powerful forces within the Church, who favor accommodation with the *Zeitgeist,* rather than Christian witness against it.

Aggiornamento is wrong for the Church, because the Church, aside from a few trivial external matters, needs no updating. Reforms in canon law and administration there may well be, but this is simply reform and not bringing up to date at all. It is the worship of the Latest Thing that I object to after all. What makes the "up to date" so right and proper and desirable, above all, for the Church?

The last century told a different story. Pius IX was no John XXIII; but he understood the crisis of the Church in his time. He did not try to adjust the Church to the then *Zeitgeist*; on the contrary, he defied the *Zeitgeist,* flinging challenge after challenge in its face. The *Syllabus of Errors* (1864) contains many things we would not agree with; but, in issuing it, Pius IX did one thing that was decisive: he made front against the spirit of his age, which was the spirit of a laic, totalistic liberalism. *No compromise,* he commanded—and we are all grateful for that today. Very shortly after, in 1865, at the *Katholikentag* of that year, Father Heinrich put his finger on the crucial point. "Medicines are often bitter," he noted, referring to the *Syllabus.* "Only when the nineteenth century is no more than a memory will mankind understand how salutary and necessary that medicine was." We understand it today.

There were many intelligent and well-meaning people in those days who deeply deplored Pius' stand, both in the *Syllabus of Errors* and in his insistence on the definition of the dogma of Papal Infallibility at the First Vatican Council (1869-1870). Some, including the omniscient editors of the *New York Tribune,* even predicted the end of the Church within a few decades: how could any institution survive that was so benighted as to defy the "modern spirit"? Well, the "modern spirit" of those days has come and gone; but the Church remains in unparalleled strength, not least (humanly speaking) for old Pius' "reactionary" obstinacy in preventing the Church from chasing after the *Zeitgeist.*

The Church must indeed "take account" of contemporary trends in intellectual and social life, "taking account" of contemporary trends however, does not necessarily imply surrendering to them: but that is precisely what the slogan *aggiornamento* invites us to do.

As I write these lines, I note that, at last, Rome is speaking. A Religious News Service dispatch, during the first week of April, informs us that:

> Pope Paul VI, speaking in unusually forthright terms, rebuked elements in the Catholic Church that "seem to have nothing else to give Catholic life, than bitter, destructive, and systematic criticism . . . Pope Paul . . . chided "those who throw doubt upon, or deny, the validity of the Church's traditional teachings so as to invent an untenable

theology," and "those whose tastes seem to lie in creating contrary currents of opinion and sowing suspicion, thus undermining trust and docility to authority and laying autonomous claims devoid of foundation or wisdom.

[He castigated] also those who, to be modern, find everything fine and worthy of imitating that they find elsewhere, while everything is intolerable, open to dispute, or old-fashioned that they find in their own fields.

What the Church needs today is not incitement to *aggiornamento;* but—I dare say it—another, hopefully more adequate, more intelligent and discriminating, *Syllabus of Errors* for our time.

The Ideology of Aggiornamento

THOMAS MOLNAR

What goes these days by the name of "updating" or *aggiornamento* within the Roman Catholic Church is, in its bulk and basic inspiration, the ecclesiastical counterpart of the political "opening to the left."

Like de Gaulle, Nasser, Sukarno, etc., the Vatican has interpreted American—and Western—behavior in the past twenty years as a sign of abdication from global responsibility. Communism is here to stay, a powerful Catholic minority holds. It will, like a bulldozer, first level Europe then America; hence it is imperative to establish a *modus vivendi* with it, or, in more fashionable terms: peaceful coexistence. The Church's task is to conquer the conqueror, writes Carlo Falconi, an ex-priest representing a group of Italian priests and laymen, "to baptize those who want to and may well in fact bury us."

This involves more than just concordats signed with Hungarians and Poles, more than efforts to rid Budapest of the embarrassing presence of Cardinal Mindszenty. It involves coming to terms with the "progressive" left-wing circles that live in symbiosis with Marxism and constitute the bridge towards the Communist world: worker-priests, Teilhard de Chardin, Florence's ex-mayor La Pira and, closer to home, Catholics for common worship with Protestants, nuns, and priests rioting over Vietnam, and the neo-obscurantists of *Ramparts* Magazine.

The core argumentation sounds like this: after the

Council of Trent the Church conducted an aggressive policy in harmony with the age of absolutism and the nation state. From Pius IX (promulgator of the *Syllabus of Errors*) to Pius XII the Church chose to live in a cold war climate. Pius XII was as aggressively anti-Communist (see the play, *The Deputy*) as Stalin was anti-Western. However, the argument runs, we live in a different world now; peace and coexistence are possible; the Church is no longer threatened because mankind's overwhelming common aspiration is peace, world rule of law, and prosperity. The Church should make friends among all faiths, even among atheists. It should be in the forefront of the real battle of the century: for social and economic well-being.

As for Communism, certain French and Italian priests advocate dialogue on all occasions, common electoral lists, united efforts to bring about a better world through mutual concessions. Examples: the French Catholic boy scout, now clad in red shirt, his organization re-named, Communist-fashion, "Pioneers," is taught not to be patriotic, but "social-minded." The film on Jesus by the Italian Communist Pasolini, is shown in Notre Dame of Paris and awarded a Catholic film prize. *Ramparts'* editor, Edward Keating, organizes pickets in behalf of *The Deputy* in New York, praises riots against HUAC and Vietnam policy alongside leftist student groups.

Only in this pre-revolutionary climate can we understand the other manifestation of *aggiornamento* ideology, less sharply focused but equally devastating to the faith, and demoralizing to the faithful. Keep in mind that a basic tactic of Communists is to find and exploit the so-called contradictions inherent in the enemy camp: bourgeois society, the free-enterprise system, racial tension in the U.S., colonialism—and now the Church. So it is that the leftist newspapers never tire of contrasting the "reactionaries" in the Curia with the "progressives" —Cardinals Frings, Suenens, Alfrink, etc. How easily are the latter identified with the "forces of history," the former with backwardness and "medieval" attitudes! One group is aligned with *good* Pope John XXIII, and the other with *bad* Pope Pius XII.

For years now great numbers of the French clergy and hierarchy have supported *Pax*, the state-sponsored

"Catholic" organization in Poland (recently revealed to be simply a branch of the police apparatus). This served to discredit and demoralize Catholics in Poland and to create dissension in France itself among the Catholic partisans and opponents of *Pax*. Cardinal Wyszynski himself finally begged Catholics in the West "not to make the cross the Poles are carrying heavier still."

Communist propaganda among France's Catholics has been strikingly successful. The "progressives," heartened by the turns Vatican II has taken, have become more brazen, imagining that History is on their side. The "integrists" (conservatives), however, have fought back vigorously, most recently with the publication of a sensational best-selling novel by Michel de Saint-Pierre, *The New Priests,* that vigorously denounces revolutionaries within the Church. The progressives riposted in *Temoignage Chretien,* with a bitter review by a priest who called all readers of the book "dogs". This prompted the heart-rending cry of Edith Delamare: "Our priests hate us!"

The American reader may discount these clashes; feel that they are deplorable but that they do not affect the heart of the problem which is that the Church needed up-dating. These battles could easily be dismissed as confined to the French and Italian clergy and laity, both of which are traditionally noisy and occasionally rude. Until one realizes the extent to which American Catholic thinking has been influenced by the works of "progressive" French theologians.

The message of these works and of shallow popularizers like Teilhard de Chardin is clear: the Church has followed the wrong track; now it must adopt the new spirit. The Church has been "militant"; now it must renounce its distinguishing signs and join other religions on equal terms: not hold itself the "true Church," but recognize the equality of other creeds and create with them a common front against colonialism, under-development, and the bomb. As several priests have replied to critics, we must now preach more important things than God: concern for civil rights, adequate housing. In short, the secular gospel.

Those who condemn "triumphalism" wish to combat the Popes' supremacy; downgrade liturgical and cere-

monial brilliance (depriving the faithful of esthetic uplift
and joy); to do away with the preponderance of Latin
—in a world they themselves call small and in which
traveling Catholics will in future be unable fully to participate in Masses celebrated in the vernacular. Those
who, in the name of "modernism," wish to put priests
and nuns in worldly garb forget that the renunciation
and sacrifice-seeking part of our being is thirsty for
distinctness and, yes, the outward marks of such sacrifice as celibacy, chastity, poverty.

Let's face it: the ideologues of the *aggiornamento* are
champions of the Church's fragmentation and dilution.
They want to destroy the delicate balance between monarchy, aristocracy and democracy within the Church;
they preach, in short, its "Protestantization." I do not
say this in any pejorative sense. In fact, serious Protestant clergymen (and Jewish rabbis) have expressed concern about the sudden folly and self-debasement of these
Catholic ideologues, warning that dialogue should not
mean surrender—on either side! In this they show more
decorum than hosts of Jesuits, than Thomas Merton re-
verting to his earlier leftist sympathies, than shock-troop
theologians like Hans Kung, rushing to board what they
consider the bandwagon of victory. They agitate for a
scientific religion, for the elimination of "historical accretions and folklore," and for the "dis-alienation" of
man so that he may become, like the Marxist ideal, a
purely earthly being.

The people, that is, the great majority of ordinary
Catholics, resist the cutting winds of this sharp opening
to the left; they point out the dangers of committing the
Church to a Teilhardian theology based on an already
dated evolutionism; they answer in Latin to the priest's
vernacular; they challenge progressive theologians at
public debates and chase from the rostrum the French
and Swiss editors of *Information Catholiques Interna-
tionales* who still defend the *Pax*-facade of the Polish
NKVD. But many Catholics are intimidated too, like
some country curates in France. Art critic Andre Chas-
tel regretfully reports that, to combat "triumphalism" in
Church art, some priests are burying precious medieval
retables and altar pieces and saying Mass at a kitchen
table.

The image of interred art treasures through which past and more secure ages glorified the faith, is a sign that the real Church may be forced once again down into the catacombs while the *aggiornamento*-ideologues parade above their show-off simplicity and folksy ecumenism. The poor priest who now hides the artistic beauty of past ages is acting in the spirit of these ideologues who, with their Marxist-materialist commitment, command that working class neighborhoods build churches that look like factories. The Church, they say, should not "triumphantly" assert its splendor. But why should it not? The working man, like everyone else, wants to celebrate his meeting with God in beautiful surroundings, not in the language he uses and abuses all week, but in Latin which promotes his festive mood. But the leveling, debasing ideologue, Catholic and non-Catholic, cares very little for the ordinary man: his concern is for fellow-intellectuals.

So the *aggiornamento* party advances, hoping to meet its brothers of the world revolution halfway: in common worship of the UN and totalitarian world government at Point Omega. It argues, of course, that it is through this alliance that the Church will undermine, from within, the world Communist movement, and engage in an up-to-date form of proselytizing as in the days of the Roman Empire 1,600 years ago.

But isn't such a claim ludicrous? Christianity conquered not when Rome was at her zenith, under Caesar and Augustus, but 300 years later, when it was in decline. Communism will also decline—centuries or perhaps decades, from now. But at present it is still the stronger ideology. The proof is that it never apologizes, and always conquers. Its leaders, although occasionally thwarted in some of their designs, know what they want and push ahead even when delays occur in their timetable.

The Catholic Church could combat them only by emphasizing the irreconcilable differences, and by showing equal firmness toward the progressive camp of Catholics and non-Catholics alike. But a vacillating Vatican that tolerates agitating nuns, Jesuits slandering the Pope, red-shirted "Pioneers," confirms the correctness of Lenin's strategy: "To finish off with religion it is much more important to introduce the class struggle within the Church, then to attack directly religion itself."

Who is Accommodating to What?

L. BRENT BOZELL

Within the article of faith that it will, in some earthly
dimension, survive, I doubt whether one can exaggerate
the trouble the Church is in. That is, of course, an *a
priori* judgment: the mounting evidence of disarray,
however dispiriting, could not in itself warrant historical
pessimism in the light of the Church's demonstrated
capacity for digging herself into and out of bigger
messes than any that have brought empires down. What
is different about the current disorders is that they are
unattended by assurances that their perpetrators conceive
Christianity as a *giver* of norms for judging the secular
realm, rather than the other way around. What justifies
alarm is the widespread willingness in the Church (eagerness is the word, of course, for the *avant garde*) to con-
sult mirrors arranged by Christianity's enemies, so defined
both by history and theology.

Pope Paul's first encyclical, *Ecclesiam Suam,* was
plainly addressed to this, the most fundamental of disorders. But where it was not denounced as retrograde,
the encyclical seems to have been dismissed as a venture
in triviality. Why? There is much that is spineless in
the uncritical embrace of *aggiornamento,* a recognizable
tolerance for intimidation. Above all, however, the new
enthusiasms have revealed an other-directedness in the
bosom of the Church—a longing to be free of itself, to
be liberated from the constraints imposed by a specifically Christian apostolate. In other ages, the heart of the

Church, for all its worldly distractions, was content with
saving souls, an opportunity regarded as infinitely rich
and expanding, notwithstanding that the means were
understood to be static: the teaching of its own Truth,
and providing conduits of Grace. Today the Church
feels drawn to broader and more exciting horizons.
Where these horizons lie, the innovators candidly profess
not to know. But neither, it seems to me, have they
paused to ponder whence the beckons come.

The striking thing about the innovations in Catholic
thought is that they are innovations to no one but Catholics. The fresh air John XXIII is said to have let into
the Church has understandably intoxicated the Catholic
Left, by wafting away many of its frustrations; but for
the rest of the world it is—all of it—very stale stuff.
That is why the new enthusiasm is primarily an amuse-
ment to non-Catholics, and a welcome one to the foes of
Catholic pretensions, who, whatever else they may have
thought of the Roman Church, have never before had
the pleasure of regarding it condescendingly. Consider
the fresh ideas, still unanointed to be sure, that now
blow freely out of the editorial offices of the Catholic
press and down the corridors of the seminaries; population control and planned parenthood via contraceptive
artifacts; mixed marriages with parents invited to slug
it out over the children's souls, on an equal footing;
proscription of capital punishment; a "dialogue" with
homosexuals; nuns dressed like all the other ladies;
priests as family men; religious liberty, meaning, con-
cretely, an Open Door policy for Spain; racial equality
as the age's transcendent moral command (opposition
to racial discrimination, according to the editor of a
diocesan weekly, "takes temporary priority over all
other obligations including ecumenism, and worship of
God because of present conditions"); accommodation as
the relevant mode of dealing with Communists; the
preeminance of the social gospel (the Catholic twist: a
holy war on poverty); the possibilities of constructing a
theology on a study of fossils. These are the principal
items of the current diet, pejoratively stated perhaps.
The point, however, is not that they are bad ideas, or
imprudently advanced, but that as a matter of record
every one of them has its ancestry in the preoccupations

of a world that has always viewed itself as laying siege at the walls of Rome. The point does not by itself disprove the thesis that *aggiornamento* is divinely inspired; it does corroborate the intuition that it is Caesar, not the Holy Ghost, who has a corner on the attentions of a large part of the contemporary Church.

The corporate Church, as distinct from the noisy little magazines, has formally embraced very few of the specifics of *aggiornamento*. The tendencies are nonetheless unmistakable. The bringing of the liturgy down to the meeting house level is more than a case in point, for the motivations for the changes betray the emergence of a whole set of priorities in which adjustment to secular norms (in this case primarily psychological and sociological) plays the leading role. The reigning apologetics have much to say about "renewal," the purging of historical accretions, a return to the primitive ways; but this is window-dressing, and especially unconvincing as part of a great movement to bring the Church up to date. Collective effusions tailored to the most pedestrian modes available bear a less obvious relation to the practices of the early Christians than to the insights of the group psychologists, the rationalists and the equalitarians for whom Person, and Mystery, and Majesty are obstructions to be overcome. An urge to make the Church acceptable to Protestants is also recognizable in some of the new forms. (The implied insult to Protestants in this connection has not been sufficiently noted: believing in private judgment, the separated brethren would presumably look with greater favor on *individual* conversions.)

But the alleged "Protestantization" of the liturgy has been over-emphasized: the innovators do not wish so much to imitate Luther, as to generate a world mood that will forget that Luther and his opponents had differences. The tendency of modern ecumenism is to blur distinctions at every level of human thought and experience, which is not Protestantism but Hinduism.

I have gone as far as I care to without the counsel of experts who may spot, even in agony, pride. So far I am sustained by the instruction of the New York Jesuit, who has taught philosophy at Yale, that "obedience can never be unquestioning"—that the relationship between authority and subject should reflect "the image of conversation." This appears, however, to cut in two ways, at least in the experience of the Rev. Gommar De Pauw who, having launched the Catholic Traditionalist Movement, had a conversation last week with the Cardinal of Baltimore which had as its result the preemptory termination of that particular questioning.

Some of the
Pope's Problems

ALICE-LEONE MOATS

When Pope John XXIII first announced that he intended to hold an Ecumenical Council, one of its primary purposes was said to be the promotion of Christian unity. Vatican experts assumed that the promotion of Christian unity was aimed at forming a strong alliance of Roman Catholics, Orthodox Catholics and Protestants to combat Communism and the atheism and materialism so sedulously spread throughout the world by the Kremlin and its agents. Nobody—not even the Communists —foresaw that some of the by-products of the council would be: 1) an opening to the left by the Christian Democrats in Italy; 2) a warm welcome for Khrushchev's daughter and son-in-law by John XXIII in his private apartments; 3) the establishment by Paul VI of a Secretariat, which according to newspaper accounts is to start dialogues with atheists, agnostics and skeptics.

It is difficult to explain exactly how all this came about. Still, it is possible to isolate some of the factors causing the surprising changes that have taken place recently in Rome.

One of the most important factors has been neglected in the many analyses of Vatican policy written since 1960; the role played by Washington during the Kennedy Administration. It is no secret that the Christian

Democrats received considerable encouragement, to put it mildly, from the White House to go through with an opening to the left, but it does appear to be a secret that emissaries from Washington played a decisive part in persuading authorities at the Holy See to give their protege political party the green light, without which any plans for an opening to the left would have been still-born. My authority for this statement is a member of the Curia who was involved in the negotiations and I have been able to check it with other reliable sources. It is not really odd that John XXIII, eager to have the Church move with the times, should have been willing to accept the advice of the Catholic President of the most modern nation in the world.

There is also some basis for the rumor that the public relations methods so unexpectedly adopted by the Vatican at about that time were not thought out entirely on their own by ancient Italian monsignori in the Curia. The trouble was that they had to be carried out by the ancient monsignori who, working in a medium they didn't understand, either went too far or not far enough. The decision, for example, to keep the press informed as to what was taking place at the Council could not be criticized, but the readiness to accredit a correspondent from *L'Unita,* the Communist party organ, giving him a chance to write what could be mistaken for authoritative pieces from Vatican City, might be considered a trifle reckless.

Men trained to a strict rule of silence found it very hard to talk and the information given to the correspondents by the press office during the first session of the Council was so sketchy that everybody was forced to track down some loquacious bishop from abroad who hadn't been subjected to Vatican discipline and was willing to air his own views. Obviously, each correspondent found the source best suited to fit in with his own political attitudes or those of his newspaper. That is how matters got out of hand and the outside world was given the impression that "liberal" bishops were battling their "conservative" colleagues daily in St. Peter's. In actual fact, the lines have never been that clearly drawn.

But, the Vatican, unused to publicity, became its victim. It was taken as a hopeful sign that *L'Unita* and other Communist and leftist newspapers should show so much interest in the Council, be so sympathetic to its aims. The stunned amazement in the Vatican at the final outcome—the greatest victory the Communists had ever won at the polls—gave the measure of the naivete of the Pope and his advisers.

Shortly afterwards, John XXIII died and his place was taken by Paul VI, a man of an entirely different stamp, so enigmatic that John XXIII used to refer to him as "Our Hamlet from Milan." As an intellectual who sees two or three sides to every question, it is imposible for him to be a dictator, like Pius XII; a reserved man, it is equally impossible for him to fit the image of a pope built up in the public mind during John XXIII's reign, and the public relations mills have to grind away with no grist to feed them. He's stuck, however, with the public relations mill, with the John XXIII image, with an Ecumenical Council that was not his idea.

Since nobody understands Paul VI, nobody has ever been able to give such a clear picture of him that when a slanted story appears readers say, "That isn't true—it's out of character." Which makes it easier for certain minor Vatican officials who continue to live in the John XXIII days to give their own interpretations of any event or statement, and for correspondents to overlook or to play up what suits them. A typical example occurred shortly after Pope Paul's election when Vatican Radio came out with a strong blast against Communists, which wasn't picked up by many newspapers because someone at the Vatican press office said that the broadcast did not reflect the Holy Father's views. As it happened, the Pope had sent his personal congratulations to the author.

It is so easy to misrepresent the Pope's intentions by writing or saying too much or too little about them. The announcement that a secretariat had been formed

to deal with Communists and atheists has perhaps received the latter treatment. What seems likely is that
the new secretariat has been formed to deal with the
problems of the Catholic Church behind the Iron Curtain, not, as was implied in the announcement, to pro-
mote atheism. In that case it will perform a very useful
function that has been somewhat neglected by the Secretariat of State, where there are too few Iron Curtain experts. But if it does perform such a useful function, it
won't get any more publicity.

Reflections on
Vatican II

ARNOLD LUNN

"Many questions of the utmost importance," said the
bishop who was having tea with us in a flat lent to us
in Rome by a kind friend, "have been discussed by this
Council but when a friend of mine, Father X, returned
for a week to London, the only question he was asked
was 'Will the Council change Catholic teaching on birth
control?' "

During the weeks I spent in Rome the unofficial comments by various ecclesiastics were often more revealing
than the official pronouncements. I recorded these every
day before retiring. The reader will not, of course,
expect me to name my informants.

First as to birth control. In her long history the
Church has had few more difficult problems to solve.
The conservatives have a strong case. "How can the
Church," they maintain, "continue to claim to be a
divinely inspired guide on morals if the Church reverses
what has been her consistent teaching throughout the
centuries on one of the most important of moral problems?"

Of those who reject the Church's teaching on birth
control some continue to go to the sacraments, some go
to Mass but not to the sacraments and some give up
going to Mass. "What worries us," said a very fine priest,
"is that if the parents cease to go to Mass they won't
take the children and the whole family is lost to the

Church." "There are obviously," I said, "some cases in which nothing far short of heroic sanctity is necessary if married life is to conform to the Church's teaching." "I agree," said the priest. "Here is a case in point. A woman came to me who had twelve children, the last three deformed. I suggested that perhaps she and her husband could postpone further relations until she was past the age of child bearing. 'We have a very hard life,' she said, 'and this is one of our few pleasures. We can't give it up. Must we stay away from the sacraments?'" "I thought for some time and then said, 'I don't think that many priests would approve of the advice I shall give you but I'll take the responsibility of advising you not to stay away from the sacraments.'"

The Vatican Commission on this subject was divided, so I was told, into three groups, a) the conservatives who wanted no change, b) a group which placed great hope in the pill—a Bishop told me that a famous Catholic doctor told him that within two years an effective pill would be produced—and c) a small group which agreed with Archbishop Roberts and would allow contraception. The general view was that the discussion would continue and that there would be no definite ruling for some time.

I have what might almost be called a hereditary interest in one of the great issues before the Council, the ecumenical issue. My father, the late Sir Henry Lunn, was indeed one of the pioneers of this movement. His health broke down as a medical missionary in India, where I was born, and in 1892 he convened the first of the Grindelwald Conferences at which Anglicans and Free Churchmen met to discuss the possibility of Reunion. My father was also largely responsible for bringing about the reunion of various Methodist Churches and he took me to the meeting to celebrate the occasion. As we left after the rejoicings, he said, "My dear boy, there was a great deal more life in Methodism when the Primitive Methodists doubted the salvation of all other Methodists than there is today," a revealing comment on what may be called the ecumenical dilemma. The skeptic has some excuse for suspecting that what is bringing the churches together is an increasing doubt about the doctrines which divide them. A bishop in Rome told me that a possible convert from American Protestantism had decided to stay where he was and told the priest who was instructing him that he could see no reason to become a Catholic when the Catholic Church was becoming Protestant. What is certain is that the ecumenical movement and the increasing influence of those who like to be described as progressive Catholics has coincided with a drop in converts and vocations. One bishop told me of a priest who three years ago was instructing thirty converts and has now not one convert to instruct. Another bishop gave me very similar figures.

(I met two bishops in Rome who had no belief in anything useful coming out of the ecumenical movement, but I also met a bishop who was a great enthusiast for the movement, a convert who had given proofs in his life of his readiness to make extreme sacrifices for the Faith. "I know," he said to me, "that there has been a sad falling off of converts. That is the price we have to pay. It is, I believe, only a temporary falling off, but bishops and priests are committed to a kind of truce. If a Protestant comes to me and asks me to give my reasons for accepting the claims of the Catholic Church then I shall do my best to convert him, but a bishop who went out of his way to maintain in public that no other form of Christianity than the Catholic is fully satisfactory would be accused of being unecumenical. You, as a layman, can write what you like." "In point of fact," I replied, "my policy has been rather similar. I defended Catholicism in books consisting of an exchange of letters with the ablest enemies of the Church whom I could find, the Anglican Dr. G. C. Coulton, C.E.M. Joad and the scientist J.B.S. Haldane, but I was twice asked to preach in an Anglican Church and did so with the permission of my bishop. On one of these occasions the Anglican vicar said, "We've asked you because you have never written anything offensive about Anglicanism.")

My own views on the ecumenical movement were summed up in an article, *Ecumenism—Militant or Defeatist?* which I contributed to the *Churchman* (September 1965), an Anglican paper, in the course of which I wrote: "The problem of the ecumenist is to ensure that we retain the fervor of our own beliefs while showing greater understanding of those we do not share. Increasing tolerance must not coincide with increasing indifference. I have co-operated with an Anglican, Garth Lean, in the writing of two books, *The New Morality* and *The Cult of Softness,* in which we defended the traditional Christian beliefs and moral code. Both of us are convinced that the beliefs which we share are incomparably more important than the beliefs which separate us. Both of us believe that the ecumenical movement is of great value in so far as it is an effective and *militant* alliance between *real* Christians who are united in resistance to those who are determined to suppress not only the Christian faith but also Christian morals."

There is indeed widespread misgiving in every Church about the increasing evidence of Christian defeatism. *Herder Correspondence,* a monthly review written in English and published in Germany, and appearing also in London and New York, created a sensation by an article with the title "Have Christians Lost Their Nerve?" Most of the bishops whom I met in Rome had read this article and none was inclined to dispute its depressing conclusions. A well-known bishop told me that he was having several copies typed and sent around. He too believed that the main trouble with the Church today is lack of courage. "Catholic journalists don't want to get their fingers burnt." He feared that the ecumenical movement was taking what little was left of the fight out of the Church. "Christ said 'They will throw you out of the synagogues.' Today we priests are being invited to preach in synagogues. Too many of our Catholics are like the pale tepid lot who Dante said were not fit for Heaven and too cheap for Hell. He wasn't going to bother to speak about them. Just look at them and pass on. *'Non ragionar di lor, ma guarda e passa'.* The great word now is 'dialogue,' which means futile conversation between Christians of different communions, none of whom has any real belief in anything which he professes. Another popular word is 'encounter,' which means meeting God rather less than half way."

Today nearly a third of the world is Communist. Why? Partly because Communism was propagated by fanatic missionaries for Marxism, and even today most

Communists in the Free World are ardent propagandists for the cause, but not one Christian in a thousand makes the slightest effort to convert an atheist or agnostic. They rationalize their reluctance to master their own case, let alone propagate it, by such formulas as "Nobody is ever converted by argument, only by setting a good example." What Communists have ever said that the only way to spread Communism was by setting a good example?

Some Catholics even go further. Mr. St. John Stevas, a conservative Member of Parliament, assures us that "for the educated Catholic apologetics and polemics are out," but for Mr. St. John Stevas neither conservative apologetics nor anti-Socialist polemics are "out." It is only "uneducated" for the Catholic to state his case. No wonder that, as an eminent Catholic remarked to me, "Catholics are no longer unpopular because they've discovered that we're innocuous." The campaign for unilateral disarmament is certainly making good progress. The Editor of the *Catholic Herald* assures us Catholics are no longer satisfied with "defensive apologetics"—as if apologetics are exclusively "defensive," but demand instead "a new Christian dynamism in the fields of housing, race discrimination, social welfare and the need for developing nations." But no Christian should be *wholly* satisfied with purely secular remedies for our troubles. Christians risk no unpopularity by attacking "race discrimination," but it is increasingly unpopular to attack religious discrimination.

In Rome I discussed the religious situation in Communist countries not only with exiles but also with those who were returning to the countries in question. In Hungary the situation is perhaps improving, but according to *Communist* statistics 60 per cent of the Poles still practice their religion, but no such Pole has any hope of a successful career. They are 'second-class citizens.' A Russian, a former professor at a Russian university and an observer delegate at the Council on behalf of the Russian Church in exile, told me that Moscow would never let the Patriarch of Moscow attend as an observer. There were 1,600 churches in Moscow before the revolution. Now there are twenty. Parents are not allowed to teach religion to their children until they have reached the age of seven. In their schools they are taught that science has disproved religion and no Russian below the age of eighteen may attend Church.

There are some Catholic papers, such as the *Tablet*, which do not allow their readers to forget the plight of persecuted Christians, including Christians who are not in communion with Rome, but in general the contrast is depressing between the *esprit de corps* of Jews and Negroes and the lack of Christian *esprit de corps*. When the Jews were persecuted by the Nazis they never allowed anybody in the rest of the world to forget their plight, but today far more Christians are agitating against racial apartheid in South Africa than against religious apartheid in the Communist world. I asked a bishop in Rome if he could explain this contrast. "I am afraid," he said, "it is nothing new. When priests were being martyred in Elizabethan England there was not much concern about their fate in Rome."

The Council was responsible for great liturgical changes. The introduction of the vernacular was undoubtedly beneficial but as President of the Latin Mass Society I presented to the Pope our petition that in any church in which there is more than one daily Mass, one of these should be in Latin. It has been argued that only well-educated Catholics appreciate the Mass in Latin. This I know to be untrue but even if it were true the Universal Church in her charity should find a modest niche even for the well-educated.

The supreme problem facing not only the Catholic Church but Christianity as a whole today is the growing secularization of our world. There is indeed a concerted and effective attempt to capture the mind and culture of countries still nominally Christian for anti-Christian secularism. The Christian reaction is pitifully ineffective. Man is by nature conformist and easily intimidated by the tyranny of fashion. It is natural that he should desire to be "with it." As the contrast between the Christian and secular culture becomes more marked, the Christian is tempted to play down all that still separates him from the secularists, and to seek to conciliate a secular society by identifying himself with fashionable causes.

I remember quoting to a bishop in Rome a comment in *Herder Correspondence*—"It is surprising that since

prominent English Catholics unpopularly supported the
Franco side in the Spanish Civil War, no group representative of English Catholicism has initiated or asso-
ciated itself with an unfashionable cause, foreign or domestic. In a society which rejects and attacks much of
what Christianity stands for there must be many such
causes at hand." Authentic Christianity has always been
and will always be unpopular.

"It is curious," said the bishop, "that you should have
raised this point. I recently preached at the ordination
of a young priest. 'I hope that in your priestly career,'
I said, 'you will make many friends but if at the end of
your life you cannot recall any group which was hostile
to you you will have failed as a priest.' "

We ask: has the Vatican Council given a strong lead
to Christians and not only to Catholics who wish to cooperate for effective action against increasing secularism? Some would answer this question in the negative.
A bishop described to me a curious scene which he himself had witnessed. An African ecclesiastic whose great-
grandfather might perhaps have been a cannibal, said to
three or four bishops, of whom my friend was one,
"You can talk of nothing but the Bomb and the Pill, the
Pill and the Bomb instead of thinking how the Church
can get its message to the unconverted. 'What think ye
of Christ? Whose son is He?' You're all afraid of ideas.
But our religion began with an idea. In the beginning
was the Logos. Why don't you join with us to build a
new world, and stop all this talk about the Bomb and
the Pill. You live in fogs. We live in sunshine. When
your countries were dynamic and founding great empires, an Archbishop like Becket might get murdered
and it was unsafe to travel. Well it is not always safe
to travel in my part of the world, and an Archbishop
might still get murdered, but you have lost your empires
and are at the end whereas we are at the beginning of
something great."

"And what was the reaction of the bishops?" I asked.

"At first they said nothing and then one of them said,
'How ungrateful these Negroes are after all we have done
for them by sending them missionaries.' "

I have some sympathy with this Negro bishop's impatience but I am sanguine enough to believe that there

are good grounds for accepting the hopeful verdict of another bishop upon the achievements of the Council. This is what he said:—"This has been a great Council. The Pope has wisely allowed the eccentrics to have their say, and as the press is mainly interested in the abnormal their views have been given far more prominence than they merited, but every actual decision of the Council or statement by the Pope has been balanced. There has been no revolution but there has been real progress. Our relationship to other Churches is now on a much better basis and that is essential if real cooperation is to be achieved." (I had asked him whether effective cooperation against secularism might result from the Council.) "The real achievements of the Council cannot be judged by the public pronouncements. These are necessarily cautious but the Council has created a new spirit in the Church and what it has achieved will only become apparent as the years pass. Fifty years from now it will be recognized as having been one of the great Councils of the Church."

A recent pastoral of Cardinal Heenan's certainly provided evidence in support of the belief that the achievement of the Council should be measured less by what the bishops actually said in Rome than by what they initiate on their return to their dioceses.

VII

SOME FUN
WITH THE
DIALOGUE

Gnostics on a Train

MARVIN R. O'CONNELL

It's no fun being on the outside. I may scoff at the lodge
brother's sword and cocked hat, but deep down I'm
jealous of him, because, deep down like everybody else
I'm a snob. I often imagine myself on a train where a
man comes up to me, grasps my hand in a uniquely significant way, and makes a remark which sounds casual to
everybody in the car but me. "I'm going east," he says. (Or
sometimes he says, "I'm going west." It varies.) We look
at one another narrowly, and then, as I murmur, "I am,
too," I am suddenly flooded with a warm comradely
feeling, with a sense of belonging to a special group which
everybody in the train would like to belong to but can't.
In fact, their inability to join our society gives me particular pleasure. But, then, just as we are about to begin
a carefully coded conversation, the happy scene vanishes
and I find myself back in the cold, indifferent world
where I am just like everybody else, I suppose the difficulty is that I have never been quite able to dream up a
suitable code.

Not long ago, I took a real train trip, hoping against
hope that something would happen. And something did.

Not that anybody came up to me to tell me what direction he was traveling in. It worked rather the other way around. At the end of the coach, in two seats facing each other, sat four people, three young men and a young woman. They were talking loudly and animatedly, and my heart skipped a beat when, as I listened, I realized that they were using a code. With the thought that fate had surely brought me to the verge of a special fulfill-ment, I got out of my seat and walked to the back of the coach until I stood looking down at them.

"I'm going east," I said shyly.

One of the men looked up. "That's good" he said. "Cardinal McIntyre lives out west."

"Pardon me?"

"Cardinal McIntyre is a racist," he said pleasantly. He was a short, thickset man, about thirty or perhaps a few years younger, and was badly in need of a haircut. He wore a yellow sport shirt, oxford grey trousers and suede loafers. He held in his hand a dog-eared paperback book whose title I made out as *Encountering the Encounter*. The man turned away from me and opened the book.

"Listen to this," he said. His three companions leaned forward expectantly. "It is only in the noosphere where one can, in an existential fashion, realize the brief mo-ment of ecstasy in which involvement surges beyond the confines of experience and crashes against the shore of apathy and cant."

There was a reverential silence. Then the woman said, "What beautiful insight! Isn't it wonderful," she added brightly, "to be delivered from the syllogism."

I was struck by the intricacy of their code. Just when an outsider thought he understood what was being read or said, the meaning trailed away out of sight, like smoke rising from a cigarette. I repeated the woman's words admiringly and almost unconsciously. "What beautiful insight," I said.

"Do you really think so?" said the man who had first spoken to me. He looked at his three companions and then up to me. "Won't you join us?"

Those were the sweetest words I had ever heard. He and his companion squeezed over, and I sat down opposite the third man and the woman. I was suddenly flooded with a warm comradely feeling, with the sense of belonging to a special group which everybody in the train would have liked to belong to but couldn't. The man who had first spoken turned to me. "My name is Horace and I preside at assemblies in the Church of Rome."

"You mean you're a priest?" My enthusiasm must have been betrayed in my voice. "Well, how do you do, Father Horace. I'm a Catholic, too," and I started to bring from my pocket the rosary my mother had given me for my first Communion.

"Please," Horace grimaced, and the woman let out a long sigh. "Please, don't use those medieval expressions."

"You must have gone to a parochial school," the woman said to me. "You're obviously a victim of regimentation." She sighed again.

"Just call me Horace," Horace said. "Clerical terminology is an antiquated holdover of the post-Tridentine era," This remark, I sensed immediately, was part of the code, and so I nodded knowingly. (I hadn't had all those day dreams for nothing.) "Of course," I said.

"This," Horace continued, indicating the young man on the other side of him, "is George. George is a seminarian, a second-year philosopher."

"Down with the Curia," said George. He had short-cropped hair, eyes set rather widely apart, and soft white hands. He was afflicted with acne.

The couple across from me proved to be husband and wife: Charles was a graduate student of eight years' standing, and Rita taught third grade in a parochial school. Charles wore a thin goatee, and Rita thick, horn-rimmed glasses.

They all sat silent for a while after the introductions, and they watched me. Then Charles said, "What is it you really want? That is, what kind of involvement in your present existential situation?" He spoke with a soft lisp and looked straight over my left shoulder.

"I just want to belong," I answered.

George sucked in his lower lip, Rita sighed, and Horace ran his finger along the embroidered collar of his yellow sport shirt. "Well," Horace said, "I don't know. There are certain rules to observe, certain acclamations to be made."

"Acclamations?"

"Sure," said George. "Like Amen. You've got to get with Amen."

"Repetition is the key," Horace said, "You keep saying them over and over."

"Down with the Curia," I said.

"That's the idea." Horace looked at me with new interest.

"Clerical terminology is an antiquated holdover the post-Tridentine era."

"Say, I think he's going to be all right," George said to Rita. She took off her glasses and said, "Ah."

"Cardinal McIntyre is a racist," I said more loudly and confidently.

"But isn't it Spellman who's the racist?" asked Charles, squinting slightly.

Rita put her glasses on and turned to her husband impatiently. "Really, Charles." She almost spat the words at him. "That was last week."

"You know, Charles," George observed, "Your awareness factor is extremely low. At this rate, you'll never emerge."

Charles took a leaflet from the breast pocket of his jacket and peered at it. "It is McIntyre this week," he said ruefully.

Horace said, "Let our new friend see the list." Charles handed me the leaflet. At the top of it was the title, "Slogans for the Week," with the date, and underneath was a list of items, numbered and in bold face type. Sure enough, the first one was, "Cardinal McIntyre is a racist." I read it aloud.

Rita took off her glasses again and smiled at me. "I like you," she said. "You repeat things nice. You have a genuine sense of community." Charles colored slightly.

"Now if you want to belong to our group," Horace said to me, "the first step is to get these slogans down pat," and he shot a look of disdain at Charles.

"Karl Rahner," I read number 2, "is the greatest theologian since Buddha."

"How about that," said George, and he repeated it.

My heart sank. "I'm afraid I don't know anything about Mr. Rahner. I've never read anything of his."

"What's that got to do with it?" asked Horace.

"That's irrelevant," said Rita.

"Irrelevance," lisped Charles "is a vestige of the Counter Reformation."

"Who's got time to read books?" George demanded. "We have to keep the Johannine windows open. Karl Rahner is the greatest theologian since Buddha."

"Read the next item," said Horace.

"Liturgical plasticity is the primary objective of all men of good will." I must have shown my perplexity, because Horace looked at me sympathetically and said by the way of explanation, "The opposition of liturgical plasticity is dry legalism and rubricism, a slavery to forms which leave an empty void in the hearts of the People of God."

"Say, Horace," George asked, "is it true you prefer the zither to the guitar at the meetings of the Assembly?"

"Well," answered Horace, "I think that should be left to the primacy of the individual conscience. Just so you have bongo drums."

"I prefer the Jew's harp," said Rita. "It's so ecumenical."

"The trouble with the Jew's harp," Charles said, "is that you have to put the thing in your mouth and that makes it hard to acclaim. The same thing is true of a harmonica."

"Last Sunday," Horace said, "I presided at the Assembly from the side aisle. Next Sunday I'm going to preside from the vestibule. That way I'll have all the People of God in front of me looking the other way. That will insure their sense of community and help fill the empty void in their hearts."

"Now there's real plasticity," George commented approvingly.

"Yes, I've put wheels under the Table. You can roll it anywhere you like. We must never again be victimized by legalism."

Rita observed, "It would certainly help if we closed all the sectarian schools. They perpetuate the ghetto mentality."

"Have you closed your school yet, Horace?" Charles asked.

"No, the pastor insists on keeping it open despite the obvious fact that it has failed. Of course, what can you expect from a man who still clings to a formalism like Benediction when everybody knows that it's only 700 years old and is traceable to the irrational reaction against Arianism."

"I thought that was a midrash," said Charles, blinking twice.

"Oh, Charles," Rita exclaimed, "for Covenant's sake, can't you keep anything straight? Midrash is something that didn't happen at all. Like the three kings."

"Oh," said Charles.

"No wonder you can't pass your language requirement."

Horace seemed not to have heard this exchange. "What can you expect from a pastor who for 35 years has been obsessed with duty days, communion calls, confessions schedules, hospital visitations, sermon preparation (yes, he still calls homilies sermons), marriage counseling, catechizing, finances, maintenance, and worst of all convert classes made up of our Separated Brethren who also have the Word." George shook his head in disgust. "Maybe I can sum it up best," Horace continued, "by reminding you that when he built the plant he named it after St. Philomena. Can you beat that in the age that has produced Hans Kung?"

"Hans Kung is the greatest theologian since Buddha,"

said Charles. He looked around hopefully, but nobody paid any attention to him.

"What did your pastor think of the new name you suggested?" asked Rita.

"I don't communicate with him. He doesn't have any insights." He paused and looked wistfully at the ceiling of the coach. "But what a beautiful name: the Assembly of the Dialogue. Do you like it?" he asked me.

"Cardinal McIntyre is a racist," I answered.

"I thought you would," Horace said. "What's next on the list?"

I read from the leaflet, "The full impact of Martin Luther's insight into the genuine existential situation of divine revelation is now clear." Again I was puzzled.

"You see," George said kindly, "there couldn't be a Reformation if Martin Luther lived today."

"Why not?" I asked. I knew immediately that I had said the wrong thing. Rita turned quite pale, and Charles looked wide-eyed straight at me. I felt my face get very hot.

"Did you use the word, 'why'?" Horace spoke softly.

"Well," I stuttered, "what I meant was that I always thought Luther was a heretic." George hissed. Desperate now among all the black looks, I went on wildly. "Perhaps I'm wrong, but I thought Luther had said some things that aren't true."

"True!" snorted George, leaning toward me across Horace. "True! What are you anyway, some kind of dessicated scholastic?"

"How irrelevant can you get!" demanded Rita, shaking her little fist at me.

"I think he has an irrelevance syndrome," said Charles.

"It may be worse than that," Horace said solemnly.

"Worse?" the others chorused.

"Please listen to me," I said. "I didn't mean to say anything irrelevant. I only wanted to know what this slogan means."

"That's what I thought," said Horace. He addressed Rita, Charles and George and gestured toward me. "You

heard him. He wants to know what the slogan means."
Horace paused, and the silence grew unbearable. "Down
with the Curia," I said, but the plaintive tone in my voice
made no impression on them.

"He's guilty of non-historical orthodoxy and triumphalism," said George after a minute.

"No, George," answered Horace. "Your appreciation
of the primacy of love has made you too easy on him.
I'm afraid it's juridicism."

"Oh, no!" screamed Rita, and she scrambled past me
into the aisle. The three men followed her to the other
end of the coach, ignoring my pleas that I really hadn't
meant to ask why, that I took it all back. I was too late.
Horace snatched the leaflet out of my hand as he went
by, and so I never got the chance to hear them discuss the
fourth slogan of the week: "The present Roman legislation on birth control reflects the accumulated guilt feelings
of a celibate clergy." I have the feeling that this would
have been more interesting than the one on liturgical
plasticity.

But it was not to be. I sank deep into depression as my
journey continued, and by the time I returned home I
was on the verge of nervous collapse. It's bad enough to
be on the outside, but once you've experienced the taste
of the inner crcle, it's dreadful beyond description to be
thrust out again.

The other day I bought a cocked hat. Now I'm saving
up for a sword.

Notes Toward a Grammar

FREDERICK D. WILHELMSEN

Dialogue is in the air and on the tongue: Dialogue is topical. Let us therefore think very hard about The Dialogue and set down a list of infallible principles capable of guiding the young in search of Her Divine Essence.

1) Do not enter The Dialogue unless you absolutely have to because otherwise you may find yourself without anybody to talk to. The Dialogue does not exist in order that you might talk to somebody about something or even nothing at all. The Dialogue exists in order that you might speculate upon—Dialogue.

2) If you must *dialogue*, do not do so for apostolic reasons because the Apostles of The Dialogue tell us that apostolic motives are impure. Impurity is defined as trying to convince the other man that he is wrong and you are right. Impurity is further specified, as are all genera, by hustling the other fellow off by the scrape of the neck to *your* baptismal font. This is considered dirty pool! Don't do it!

3) Always retain the Principle of Suspended Judgement, which is German for hiding the verb until off at the end (as Willmoore Kendall might say). But please remember that once you pull the verb out of the deck and throw it on the table, you are ruled out of the game. Strothman's German Grammar will help you learn the rules.

4) Get yourself a round table (non-Arthurian however) because the circle is the perfect form for those who

want to get in shape for The Dialogue: you go round and round.

5) Sell that pulpit!

6) Remember that Aristotle defines the syllogism as the union between two insights issuing in the marriage of the conclusion. Sue for a divorce!

7) The Dialogue will insist that you submit yourself to a severe discipline in your reading habits. Until The Dialogue gets around to a Revised Edition of History, you will simply have to dub in "separated" whenever you run across "Origen was suspected of being *in h*—." Although young ladies might be shocked by such language and although children ought not to be exposed to it at all, men matured and annealed in The Dialogue find therein a test of their courage and a proof of their devotion. Folks might be separated from us but nobody, really, is in "h—."

8) The Dialogue has its preferences and you had just better learn them: If you are a Catholic, you must warm to Tillich but not to Billy Graham; if you are a Protestant, Bea is your boy but definitely not Ottaviani; if you are either a Protestant or Catholic, speak well of Will Herberg (but do not read him: he might surprise you unpleasantly).

9) The Dialogue, like all things human, has its own rhetoric, involving—as does all rhetoric—preferences: "open" against "closed"; "contemporary" against "modern"; "modern" against "medieval"; "primitive" against "civilized"; "biblical" against "scriptural"; and "scriptural" against "traditional." Our favorite word in The Dialogue is "noosphere" and our fondest enemy is "Christendom." Let no one say that The Dialogue prohibits judgments: we are all for noospheres and all against Christendoms.

10) You get one noosphere free when you sign up for The Dialogue.

11) You may use this noosphere more than once: it is good for one lecture by Hans Kung and another by Michael Novak.

12) In The Noosphere (I mean, The Dialogue) we definitely prefer time over space unless the space in question is outer space. Always speak well of time but qualify your remarks about space: otherwise you might find your-

self in a pre-Ongian universe and this would be a tragedy indeed.

13) All Enemies Within And None Without.

14) All Enemies To The Right And None To The Left.

15) In The Dialogue we never dialogue about Hungary, Poland, Lithuania, Latvia, Estonia. We prefer to seek positive values in Marxist humanism.

16) The Dialogue considers Maritain's "existentially Christian but institutionally laicist civilization" a bit out of date but will accept your copy of *Integral Humanism* or *Man and the State* as a ticket of admission to the inner sanctum of its deliberations.

17) The Dialogue likes John Courtney Murray on religious liberty but not on natural law. Bear this in mind once you begin to circulate freely inside the Temple.

18) If you are attached to the Pentagon you *may not* dialogue and there's an end to it!

19) Please remember that The Dialogue dislikes "triumphalism." It is very bad taste to triumph over anything these days. The Dialogue prefers to "maximalize."

20) Please "maximalize" all those positive values you find in secularist civilization. You know what I mean—those *positive* values surrounding you every moment in your existence.

21) Negative Principle: Do not, by any means, show any enthusiasm for the late Mr. T. S. Eliot and condemn Evelyn Waugh to oblivion: despise your past; lose your sense of humor; speak badly of Spain and Italy; hate Portugal.

22) Praise Holland.

About this book . . .

Each of the chapters presented here first appeared in *National Review* magazine, most of them in the past year. It was because of the great demand for reprints of these articles that the editors decided to collect them into one volume. Thus there is a wide variety of fact and opinion here, covering the whole range of subjects included in today's world-wide renewal of interest in religious discussion. Contributors to this book include many well-known authors and journalists, as well as some new young writers who are just establishing their literary reputations. You will find all of them capable of putting forth a strong case for their ideas — as well as striking some stinging blows at the opposition.